UK ...

and st...

ED

DOVETON

Acknowledgements

The Publishers would like to thank the following for permission to reproduce copyright materials:

The Controller of Her Majesty's Stationery Office for Figure 1 on p. 2, Figure 2 on p. 4, Figure 5 on p. 26, Figure 10 on p. 39, Figure 11 on p. 47, Table 1 on 0. 1, Tables 2 and 3 on p. 3, Tables A and B on p. 5, Table A on p. 17, Table 4 on p. 19, Table 5 on p. 20, Table A on p. 28, and Table 6 on p. 43; Times Newspapers Ltd for the extracts on pp. 75 and 83; *The Observer* for the articles on p. 64; *The Economist* for articles on pp. 8/9, 14, 25; *The Financial Times* for the article on p. 41 and the abstract on p. 50; Longman Publishers UK for Figure 8 on pp. 36 and 37; the Bank of England for the item on p. 54; Lloyds Bank for Figure 17 on p. 85; US Department of Commerce for Figure 18 on p. 85; *Economic Review* for the article on p. 63; OECD for Figure 15 on p. 77, Table 5 on p. 60, and Tables B and C on p. 17; the Economics Association for the article on p. 80; the Commission of the European Community for the article on pp. 58/59; *The Economist* for the cartoon on p. 13; Chris Riddell for the cartoon on p. 52; the IMF for Figure 16 on p. 79; Dr Kevin Dowd for the address on pp. 86/87; Oxford & Cambridge Schools Examination Board for the questions on pp. 5, 27, 49 and 68; Associated Examining Board for the questions on pp. 15, 40, 57, 58, 68, 74, 75 and 82; Joint Matriculation Board for the questions on pp. 16/17, 28, 40 and 58; University of London Examinations and Assessment Council (formerly University of London School Examinations Board) for the questions on pp. 15/16, 28, 40, 58, 75, 82 and 83; University of Oxford Delegacy of Local examinations for the questions on pp. 16, 58 and 82; Welsh Joint Education Committee for the questions on pp. 49 and 50; University of Cambridge Local Examinations Syndicate for the question on p. 49; Southern Universities Joint Board for the question on p. 68.

The Publishers have made every effort to contact the correct copyright holders. However, if any material has been incorrectly acknowledged, the Publishers would be pleased to make the necessary arrangements at the earliest opportunity.

UK trade and sterling

Charles Smith

*Brynteg Comprehensive School,
Bridgend, Mid Glamorgan*

Series Editor
Bryan Hurl
Head of Economics, Harrow School

This book is dedicated to Maria Garcia López, late of Calle Ecuador, Vigo, Spain; known as Señora Maruja to the children of the 'Casablanca' district, and as Tía to her family in Wales.

Heinemann Educational Books Ltd.

Halley Court, Jordan Hill, Oxford OX2 8EJ

OXFORD   LONDON   EDINBURGH
MELBOURNE   MADRID   ATHENS
BOLOGNA   PARIS   SYDNEY
AUCKLAND   SINGAPORE   TOKYO
IBADAN   NAIROBI   HARARE
GABORONE   PORTSMOUTH NH (USA)

First published 1992

British Library Cataloguing in Publication Data

A catalogue record for this book is available from the British Library

ISBN 0 435 33016 0

Typeset and illustrated by Taurus Graphics, Abingdon, Oxon.

Printed and bound in Great Britain by Clay Ltd, St Ives plc.

Contents

Preface

It is far too easy to take for granted this core topic area of trade. Pause and consider, then, what this experienced teacher and examiner is offering you here as he challenges the received wisdom of the average text:

- Are the standard reasons for protectionism actually tenable?
- Is a persistent balance of payments problem a cause for concern?
- Does inflation wipe out the competitive advantage of devaluation?
- Can you prove, not merely assert, the Marshall-Lerner principle?

Charles Smith has provided an attractively presented, well illustrated and stimulating text that puts UK trade and sterling at the forefront of teaching Economics in the 1990s.

Bryan Hurl
Series Editor

Acknowledgement

I wish to thank the Series Editor, Bryan Hurl, for his encouragement and advice; Sue Walton and the Heinemann team for their support; and Julia, Sally and Matthew Smith for their patience. I must also thank the many students who have belonged to my classes over the years: if I know anything about teaching Economics, they have taught me most of it.

C.S.

Chapter One
UK plc

'*For the times they are a-changing.*'   Bob Dylan

International trade

What is international trade? According to the *Penguin Dictionary of Economics* it is:

> ... the **exchange** of goods and services between one country and another. The exchange takes place because of differences in costs of production between countries, and because it increases the economic welfare of each country by widening the range of goods and services available for consumption.

Where trade is in a physical commodity it is classed as **visible trade**; and when it is in services such as banking, tourism and insurance it is classed as **invisible trade**.

The UK was the first country to undergo an 'industrial revolution', and during the nineteenth century became known as the 'workshop of the world'. During the late nineteenth and early twentieth centuries the pattern of industry in the UK followed a path which is very familiar to economists, with the secondary sector (manufacturing) producing a larger proportion of domestic output and employing a larger proportion of the working population than the primary sector. Since the Second World War the tertiary (service) sector has grown to become the largest. In international terms, this has been frequently reflected by a deficit in visible trade which was in a sense 'financed' by the certainty of an invisible trade surplus. Manufacturing now produces only 25 per cent of the gross domestic product (GDP), and to some economists UK plc is now a 'post-industrial' economy.

Table 1 The UK balance of payments on the current account between 1984 and 1991 (£ million)

1984	1985	1986	1987	1988	1989	1990	1991*
1811	2878	187	−4159	−15 520	−20 404	−15 200	−6 015

* First three quarters only
Source: *Economic Trends*, December 1991

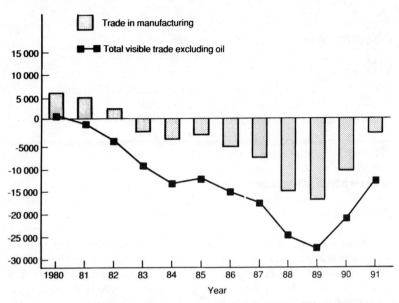

Figure 1 Trade balance and manufacturing (£ million, current prices)

After the Second World War the UK experienced economic growth and a general rise in living standards on a scale unknown by any previous generation. At the same time, however, there was a relative decline in economic performance when compared with other western countries. In 1950 the UK sold 25 per cent of the world's manufactured exports, but by the 1980s this fell to less than 9 per cent. During the mid-1970s, North Sea oil was hailed as a major national asset, yet by the late eighties and early nineties the UK balance of payments had begun to show record deficits (see Figure 1 and Table 1). How can the UK seriously claim to be a businesslike 'enterprise economy' if, unlike a business enterprise, it cannot 'balance' its books?

Table 1 shows an important change, between 1986 and 87, when the balance of payments moved into overall deficit.

What goods and services does the UK trade in?

In the mid-1980s some commentators suggested that the workshop of the world had become a 'service centre'. Others, such as George Wright, an official of the Transport and General Workers Union (TGWU), claimed that Britain was becoming a 'coolie economy', whose manufacturing base had been replaced by 'screwdriver operations' – whereby Japanese and American firms gained access to the lucrative European market by employing a British workforce to assemble components designed and manufactured elsewhere.

On a prime-ministerial visit to the Metro shopping centre in County Durham in 1986, Mrs Thatcher claimed that developments such as retail malls and fast food outlets would become major employers in the future. Critics suggested that a prime error of the Thatcher years was a failure to recognize that the demand for manufactured goods in the UK is just as strong as for services (see Tables 2 and 3), and that the building of retail parks selling largely imported goods to satisfy a 'boom' in demand financed by easily available (but expensive) credit facilities was an exercise in short-termism of the highest order.

Table 2 UK visible trade in 1990 (£ million)

	Exports	Imports	Balance
Food, beverages and tobacco	6 990	11 610	−4 620
Basic materials	2 248	5 528	−3 280
Oil	7 451	5 933	1 518
Other mineral fuels and lubricants	324	1 455	−1 131
Semi-manufactured goods	28 875	31 565	−2 690
Finished manufactured goods	53 879	62 629	−8 750
Commodities and transactions not classified according to kind	2 271	1 993	278
Totals	102 038	120 713	−18 675

Source: *UK Balance of Payments* (Pink Book), 1991

Table 3 UK trade in services in 1990 (£ million)

	Credits	Debits	Balance
General government	432	2 753	−2 321
Private sector and public corporations			
Sea transport	3 847	3 591	256
Civil aviation	4 358	4 674	−316
Travel	7 784	9 916	−2132
Financial and other services	15 649	5 935	9 714
Totals	32 070	26 869	5 201

Source: *UK Balance of Payments* (Pink Book), 1991

Who are the UK's trading partners?

Figure 2 shows the growing significance of the European Community (EC) over the last quarter of a century. There has been a remarkable

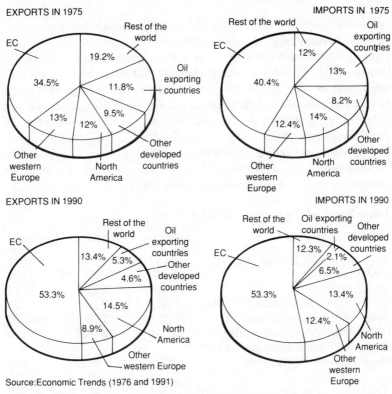

EXPORTS IN 1975

IMPORTS IN 1975

EXPORTS IN 1990

IMPORTS IN 1990

Source:Economic Trends (1976 and 1991)

Figure 2 Britain's trading partners in 1975 and 1990

change. In 1975 many commentators were still convinced that Britain could leave the EC and forge closer links with the USA and the countries of the British Commonwealth. In September 1991, when Mrs Thatcher suggested the creation of an 'Atlantic Free Trade Area', her comments had a quaint nostalgic ring to them and were largely ignored. Neither the UK government nor its opposition parties can now seriously contemplate a disengagement from Europe, with the EC accounting for over half of UK trade and the single market now with us.

An enterprise economy?

Lord Young, who was a member of the UK government for much of the 1980s, attempted to characterize his time in politics as 'the enterprise years'.

To what extent does a country's trading position have to be like that of an enterprise? Does a country need to operate with a 'surplus' in the same way as a business needs to make a profit? Do balance of payments deficits really matter? These are questions to which we shall return.

```
┌─────────────────────────────────────────────────────────┐
│                      KEY WORDS                            │
│                                                           │
│   Exchange                   Invisible trade              │
│   Visible trade              Enterprise                   │
│                                                           │
└─────────────────────────────────────────────────────────┘
```

Reading list

Feinstein, C., 'British economic growth: international and historical perspectives', *Economic Review*, May 1990.

National Institute of Economic and Social Research (NIESR), Chapter 1 in *The UK Economy*, Heinemann Educational, 1990.

Paisley, R. and Quillfeldt, J., Exercise 8 in *Economics Investigated*, Collins Educational, 1989.

Data Response Question 1

The UK balance of payments

This task is based on a question set by the Oxford & Cambridge Schools Examination Board in 1991. Study Tables A and B, which are extracted from *CSO Economic Trends*. Account for and comment on the trends shown in the tables.

Table A Visible and invisible trade figures (£ million)

	Visible trade			Invisible trade			
	Oil	non-oil	Total	Services	IPD	Transfers	Total
1985	8 101	−11 233	−3 132	6 606	2 721	−3 034	6 293
1986	4 069	−13 433	−9 364	6 253	5 210	−2 136	9 327
1987	4 183	−15 112	−10 929	5 667	4 824	−3 385	7 106
1988	2 787	−23 613	−20 826	4 186	5 513	−3 545	6 154
1989	1 481	−24 593	−23 112	3 960	4 643	−4 558	4 045

Table B The balancing item (£ million)

	Current account balance	Net transactions in UK external assets and liabilities	Balancing item
1985	3 161	−7 885	4 724
1986	−37	−9 868	9 905
1987	−3 823	−6 185	10 008
1988	−14 672	4 155	10 517
1989	−19 067	4 043	15 024

Chapter Two

Trade theory

'*He who had received the five talents went at once and traded with them; and he made five talents more. So also, he who had the two talents made two talents more.*' Gospel according to St Matthew 25: 16–17

International trade and domestic trade

International trade takes place *between* countries, while domestic trade takes place *within* countries. How does trade between the UK and Spain compare with trade between Cardiff and Newcastle?

Similarities

In a sense, there is no such thing as trade between *nations* or *cities*. What actually happens is that trade takes place between persons. These persons might be individuals, or they might represent businesses or other institutions (including, sometimes, departments of central or local government). Thus, when we say that trade takes place between Cardiff and Newcastle, or between the UK and Spain, what we really mean is that goods and services are exchanged between individuals and institutions which happen to be located in these various places.

Secondly, all trade takes place because of *specialization*. The theory underlying international trade is an extension of principles which influence the division of labour and the localization of industry. People specialize, regions specialize and countries specialize as a result of the principle of **comparative advantage** or the law of **comparative costs**. This is further discussed below.

Thirdly, specialization is related to the idea of *factor immobility*. It is easier to move the output of factors of production than it is to move the factors themselves. For example, it is easy to trade in coal; it is impossible to transplant coal mines.

Differences

Usually, *distances* are longer when international trade is compared with domestic trade, although of course this is not always the case.

London is closer to Dieppe than it is to Liverpool, although because of the sea crossing the *transport costs* involved in reaching Dieppe might be higher.

Secondly, there may be *economic, social* and *cultural* differences, which in effect add to the costs of international trade. There may, for example, be language differences which necessitate expenditure on translation facilities. There may also be variations in weights and measures, different time zones and even office hours. Perhaps most significantly of all, international trade is likely to require an exchange of currencies.

Thirdly, the *risks* involved in international trade might well be greater than those experienced in domestic trade. Businesses find themselves dealing with distant customers and markets, whose reliability might be unknown, or countries prone to natural disasters or political instability. Because of the distances involved and consequent time delays, there may be *liquidity* problems: firms will need longer-term credit in order to finance their foreign trade deals, and might need extra insurance cover in order to hedge some of the extra risks involved.

Fourthly, international traders are more likely than domestic traders to suffer from *barriers to entry*, the most obvious of these occurring when goods are subject to inspection at customs posts. Customs inspections between certain countries such as the trading bloc formed by the EC might be no more than a minor irritation with a cost in terms of time delays, or they might represent more significant barriers to free trade, such as tariffs, quotas or prohibitions imposed by governments for protectionist reasons.

Why does international trade take place?

David Ricardo (1772–1823) was the first economist to show clearly how international trade depended on the law of comparative costs. This law states:

> *Countries will specialize in the production of those items in which their comparative advantage is greatest.*

In order to understand this principle, we must first distinguish between comparative advantage and **absolute advantage**.

A country has an *absolute advantage* over another in the production of a commodity if, with a given amount of resources, it can produce more of that commodity than the other country. A country has a *comparative advantage* over another in the production of a commodity if it can produce that commodity at a lower opportunity cost than the other country.

This was a very subtle and important insight on Ricardo's part, because comparative advantage is independent of absolute advantage, and is often far less obvious. The reading list at the end of this chapter contains texts which use a simple numerical example (usually involving two imaginary countries each capable of producing two commodities) to show how total world output (and hence world income and living standards) can increase if countries specialize in those commodities in which they have a comparative advantage. Such models also show that, depending on the **terms of trade** (the ratio of export prices to import prices), all participants in international trade can gain by giving up their **self-sufficiency**, so becoming interdependent with other countries and trading with them.

The relevance of comparative and absolute advantage to contemporary debate is discussed in the accompanying boxed article from the *Economist* entitled 'Trade made the ship to go'.

Trade made the ship to go

In the days when clippers raced across the oceans, the point of trade was as clear as the ships were beautiful. They sailed to Japan, or China, or Australia loaded with something that Britain had and the Japanese wanted, and returned with tea, silk or wool. These merchants did not speak in the way George Bush did in Japan on January 7th–10th: that we buy your cars so you should buy ours. Silk for silk: not a very worthwhile trade. Nor did they speak as Japan and the European Community are doing about farm trade, ahead of a crucial meeting on January 13th in GATT's Uruguay round of trade negotiations: that we cannot buy your rice and wheat because our farmers cannot grow them as cheaply as yours can. Tea too cheap to buy: such talk would have deserved a keelhauling.

The false problem is the view that Japan is an unfair trader. It is not. Its formal and informal barriers to trade are, on average, lower than in other industrial countries. What is true, however, is that Japanese businessmen are like businessmen everywhere – protectionist when it suits their interests. When developing a new product or nurturing sales of an old one, Japanese producers will try to get their market protected against competition. Their closeness to the relevant ministries – usually the Ministry of International Trade and Industry, or that for telecommunications – means that they sometimes get away with it. That is why there are so many anecdotes about closed markets, ranging from the comical to the outrageous. But anecdotes do not add up to a general truth. More often than not, the producer lobbies do not get their way. When they do, as over Japan's ban on rice imports, it is good for the lobbies, but not for Japan as a whole.

If Japan is so open, why doesn't it import? The answer is that does, hugely. In 1990 it was the world's third-largest importer, taking in $235 billion-worth of goods. Its imports were thus bigger than the GNP of Sweden, and almost as large as that of India; since 1985 they have risen by 84%. Whereas in 1980 only 23% of those imports were manufacturers, by 1990 the proportion had risen to more than half. Measured by imports per head, Japan is pretty similar to America: $1,900 in 1990 against America's $2,050.

The point of trade is to allow an economy to specialise. If a country is better at making ships than sealing-wax, it makes sense to put more resources into ship-building, and to export some of the ships to pay for imports of sealing-wax. This is even true if it is the world's best maker of sealing-wax, for it will still prosper by making ships instead – which, in turn, is why countries can trade successfully even if they are not best at anything. This is what David Ricardo, a British economist in the early 19th century, meant when he coined the term "comparative advantage". That phrase is now one of the most misused of economic ideas, since it is often wrongly assumed to mean an advantage compared with other countries (as in "soon America will not have a comparative advantage in anything"). This matters for more than merely semantic reasons, for Ricardo's insight was a powerful one.

To Ricardo, Japan's adversarial trade would have been entirely explicable. It is good at making cars, so it specialises in that and exports a lot of them; imported cars find it hard to compete, unless they are a different sort of car (like a BMW); Japan uses the export revenue to buy lots of things it is less good at making, such as drugs and aeroplanes. It does not require trade barriers to achieve this result: markets and relative prices do the trick. Where government blocks trade, as with rice, it traps resources in an area in which Japan is inefficient.

Carving up markets between car makers, or any other producers, thwarts that process of specialisation through trade. So does spending billions on protecting West European or Japanese farmers; those billions could bring more European or Japanese prosperity if they were spent elsewhere. So would scuppering the Uruguay round, for the point of agreeing common trade rules is to allow comparative advantage to work its magic. Those who sailed in the clippers would not have recognised the phrase, but they certainly knew what it meant.

Source: *The Economist*, 11 January 1992

How do countries acquire a comparative advantage?

Let us consider why it is that some countries are more efficient than others at producing certain goods and services.

Firstly, this might be due to *natural factor endowments* which are usually beyond the control of an individual country. The UK, for instance, can produce coal and crude oil more readily than France, simply because it has been endowed by nature with deposits of these minerals, which are lacking in France. Why, on the other hand, does Japan appear to be more efficient than the UK at car manufacturing? This is largely due to differences in past *investment*; Japan has devoted resources towards building up its productive capacity, and in acquiring the *knowledge and skills* necessary to utilize that capacity efficiently. Different countries might have different *attitudes* towards things such as long-term investment, education and training; they might have different *priorities* (they might, for instance, prefer present consumption to investment for the future); they might have differently organized *institutions* (such as banks and other 'aids to trade'), different labour relations and systems of wage bargaining, and different degrees of *political stability*, all of which are among the factors which can contribute to creating and maintaining comparative advantages. Notice that comparative advantages can change over time: the UK, for instance, has succeeded in improving its ability to produce items such as steel and cars over the last ten years.

Why do countries import goods they can produce for themselves?

In a book 'of incredibly amazing facts' we can discover that Saudi Arabia imports sand! Apparently, desert sand is unsuitable for building work.

It is quite obvious why the UK does *not* need to be a net importer of oil. This is because this country possesses the natural endowment of North Sea oil. If it were not for the fact that different types of oil have different chemical compositions, and therefore can be put to different uses, then the UK would not need to import oil at all. Similarly, for many decades the UK felt no need to import any coal at all; eventually, however, foreign coal became cheaper but the government used **protectionism** to subsidize the coal industry – cheaper imports were banned until electricity privatization forced a change.

It is also fairly obvious why the UK *does* need to import bananas – it is because there is no domestic banana industry. We *could* build massive greenhouses and become self-sufficient in bananas, but the costs would be prohibitive. As an inexact generalization it can be said that it is less costly to transport the output of factors of production (bananas) than it is to relocate the factors of production themselves (banana trees).

But why does the UK import cars, when there is a domestic car industry? The answer lies at least partly in the law of comparative advantage, which we have already discussed; but given the complexity of the modern world this cannot be a complete explanation. Consumers are influenced by many considerations when selecting goods for purchase, not least of which is price; but they are also influenced by such things as styling, quality, after-sales service, and brand images created by powerfully persuasive advertising. With the growth of multinationals and monopolistic practices among producers, it is also difficult sometimes to know whether or not a car, for instance, is domestically produced or imported. And in a rapidly changing world, national boundaries themselves are tending to shift: should we in the UK regard goods from France as being imports, when both countries belong to the EC? When the Soviet Union officially became eleven separate states in December 1991, did the trade between these states change overnight from being domestic to being international?

Trade barriers

Many observers predict that in the near future the world will tend to fragment into **trading blocs,** or groups of countries trading more or less freely with each other while imposing protectionist measures against imports into the bloc. These measures might include **tariffs,** taxes on imported goods; **quotas,** physical limits on the volume of imports; or other **non-tariff barriers.** These might take the form of petty bureaucratic rules, such as the requirement that all imports are shipped

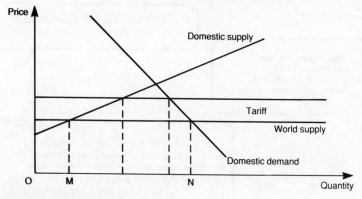

Figure 3 The effects of a tariff

through a certain port (ensuring costly delays), hidden subsidies to domestic producers, or hidden tariffs whereby indirect taxes are imposed on importers but rebated to exporters. There are also examples of **voluntary export restraints.** Japanese car manufacturers have been made to limit their exports to the EC, in the 1990s, to 11 per cent of the market (the outcome is that EC buyers pay more and the Japanese get bigger profits!). Of these methods, perhaps the main form of protection in most countries has been the tariff. Study Figure 3 before attempting the following questions:

- Explain why the world supply curve is horizontal, and why it in effect imposes a ceiling price on domestic producers if there is free trade.
- Predict the effect of a tariff on (i) domestic output (initially OM); (ii) imports (initially MN); (iii) the price paid by consumers.
- Who benefits and who loses from a tariff?

Free trade versus protection

Most economists would argue that free trade benefits everyone, by maximizing efficiency, reducing prices, increasing consumer choice,

11

and enabling economies of scale to be made. On the other hand, there are circumstances in which tariffs might be felt to be justified. The standard textbook arguments for protectionism are summarized in Figure 4, together with reasons which can be put forward to undermine each of them.

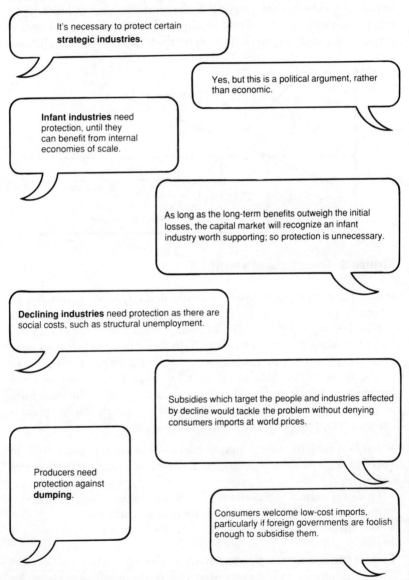

Figure 4 Arguments about protectionism

Protectionist wars – where tariffs and quotas escalate with retaliation – are not welcome, and indeed over the last few decades several international organizations have been set up to foster free trade, the most prominent of these being **GATT**, or the General Agreement on Tariffs and Trade.

GATT

This treaty was signed in 1947 by 23 industrialized nations, and since then it has expanded to a membership of 96, including a large number of newly industrialized nations, and accounting in total for over 90 per cent of the value of world trade. Since its formation there have been eight 'rounds' of negotiations leading to considerable cuts in tariffs.

GATT rules allow short-term protectionist measures to be used in certain circumstances – for instance to protect **infant industries**. GATT also attempts to remove discrimination in trade, mainly through the *'most favoured nation' clause*, which lays down that any trading concession (such as a tariff reduction) allowed by one country to another must be allowed to all member states. Being a voluntary association of nations, however, GATT cannot impose sanctions against members which disobey its rules. Neither does it have any power to force countries to allow free imports of foodstuffs, and thus the restrictions of the Common Agricultural Policy of the EC are outside the organization's terms of reference, as is trade in services.

The latest series of negotiations, known as the **Uruguay Round,** lasted from 1986 to 1990 and made only slow progress owing to the different interests of countries taking part. Newly industrialized countries attempted to broaden the scope of the talks to discuss not just tariff reductions but also restrictive trade practices (such as agricultural subsidies) or agreements on trade in textile products – 'multifibre agreements'; whereas the industrialized nations tried to turn GATT's atten-

Bring me free trade, Lord, but not yet

Any thoughts that it will be easy to turn the rising tide of trade protectionism appear to be dispelled by a new survey carried out by the *Harvard Business Review*. Some 11,700 managers in 25 countries were asked their views on the changing business world. It makes depressing reading for free-traders.

At first glance, the findings look encouraging. Asked whether there should be free trade between nations, along with minimal protection for domestic firms, 78% of American managers agreed that there should – as did 95% of German ones, 86% of Japanese, 83% of British managers… and so on.

In America especially, however, that free-trade facade swiftly cracks (see chart). of American managers, 60% believed their government should "give preference to" domestic firms when deciding what to buy; 74% reckoned the government should "actively help" those firms to succeed internationally; and 38% wanted limits on foreign ownership of corporate assets. A quarter of American managers went even further: they thought that domestic industry should be prepared to pay more for goods bought from American suppliers, and that "it should not be easy" for domestic firms to move their facilities to other countries.

British managers showed themselves to be almost as two-faced on free trade as their French counterparts; German managers were equivocal. Managers in South Korea made no pretence: only 45% of them favoured free trade and minimal protection; 70% thought their government should limit foreign ownership of Korean corporate assets; 78% believed industry should pay more to domestic suppliers in order to protect them, a peculiar view for such champion exporters.

What of Japan? On paper, it looks to be the country most committed to free trade – only 9% of Japanese managers, for instance, believed that their government should prefer to buy from Japanese companies. Either Japanese managers have been maligned or they are not telling the truth.

Managers * believing that:

governments should actively help domestic firms internationally

France	90
Britain	80
United States	74
Japan	48
Germany	40

domestic firms should be prepared to pay higher prices to domestic suppliers

Japan	33
France	31
United States	24
Britain	22
Germany	13

Source: HBR   * as % of total polled

Source: *The Economist*, 11 May 1991

tion to other topics, such as the protection of 'intellectual property'. The world's press began speculating on the very continued existence of GATT, and there appears to be some consensus that if the agreement is to survive, then it must broaden its scope and terms of reference and perhaps be given some 'teeth'. It must also face the challenge from the further integration of the Eastern European and Soviet economies into the mainstream of world trade.

KEY WORDS

Comparative advantage	Quotas
Comparative costs	Non-tariff barriers
Absolute advantage	Voluntary export restraint
Terms of trade	Strategic industries
Self-sufficiency	Infant industries
Interdependent	Declining industries
Trade barriers	Dumping
Protectionism	GATT
Trading blocs	Uruguay Round
Tariffs	

Reading list

Begg, D., Fischer, S. and Dornbusch, R., Chapter 32, part 6, in *Economics*, McGraw-Hill, 1991.

Cook, M. and Healey, N., Chapter 7 in *Current Topics in International Economics*, Anforme, 1990.

Greenaway, D., 'Gatt and multilateral trade liberalisation', *Economics*, autumn 1991.

Watts, M. and Glew, M., Chapter 1 in *International Trade in Perspective*, Hobsons Publishing, 1991.

Essay topics

1. In recent years there have been increased calls in many countries for the re-introduction of import controls. (a) What forms may import controls take? (b) Discuss the economic arguments for and against a return to trade protectionism. (Associated Examining Board, 1990)
2. Explain, in the context of international trade, what is meant by 'dumping'. Discuss whether dumping can, or should, be prevented. (Joint Matriculation Board, 1987)
3. Explain the distinction between tariff and non-tariff barriers to

trade. Discuss the likely impact of the single European market on the UK economy. (University of London School Examinations Board, 1991)

4. Does the principle of comparative advantage convincingly demolish every argument for protection? (University of Oxford Delegacy of Local Examinations, 1990)

Data Response Question 2
UK productivity
This task is based on an examination set by the Joint Matriculation Board in 1990. Study the three tables and the graphs and answer the following questions.

1. Using the data provided, compare the level and growth of productivity in the UK with that of other economies.
2. To what extent do the data support the relationship you would expect to exist in theory between changes in productivity and foreign trade?
3. How might government policies to help the UK's balance of payments position influence trends in UK productivity?

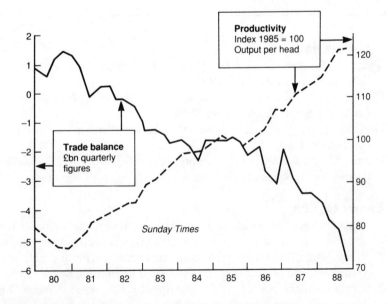

Figure A UK productivity and visible trade balance
(NB Due to data revisions there may be inconsistencies between Figure A and Table A).

Table A UK trade balances (£ million). Source: DTI

| | | Visible trade balances | | | Invisible trade |
	Current balance	Total	Oil	Total manf.	balances (total)
1970	+795	−34	−496	+2 562	+829
1971	+1 089	+190	−692	+3 015	+899
1972	+190	−750	−666	+2 145	+939
1973	−1 018	−2 586	−491	+1 488	+1 568
1974	−3 316	−5 350	−3 357	+1 970	+2 034
1975	−1 582	−3 333	−3 057	+3 737	+1 751
1976	−941	−3 959	−3 947	+4 917	+3 018
1977	−150	−2 324	−2 771	+5 886	+2 174
1978	+964	−1 593	−1 984	+5 066	+2 557
1979	−496	−3 398	−731	+2 698	+2 902
1980	+3 122	+1 353	+308	+5 450	+1 769
1981	+6 936	+3 350	+3 105	+4 576	+3 586
1982	+4 685	+2 218	+4 639	+2 297	+2 467
1983	+3 832	−1 075	+6 972	−2 448	+4 907
1984	+2 022	−4 58	+6 932	−4 054	+6 602
1985	+3 337	−2 346	+8 101	−3 151	+5 683
1986	−175	−8 715	+4 065	−5 710	+8 541
1987	−2 687	−10 162	+4 184	−7 490	+7 475
1988	−14 271	−20 336	+2 787	−14 380	+6 065

Table B Output per person employed (average annual % changes). Sources: CSO, OECD, IMF

| | Whole economy | | | Manufacturing industry | | |
	1960–70	1970–80	1980–88	1960–70	1970–80	1980–88
UK	2.4	1.3	2.5	3.0	1.6	5.2
US	2.0	0.4	1.2	3.5	3.0	4.0
Japan	8.9	3.8	2.9	8.8	5.3	3.1
Germany	4.4	2.8	1.8	4.1	2.9	2.2
France	4.6	2.8	2.0	5.4	3.2	3.1
Italy	6.3	2.6	2.0	5.4	3.0	3.5
Canada	2.4	1.5	1.4	3.4	3.0	3.6
G7 average	*3.5*	*1.7*	*1.8*	*4.5*	*3.3*	*3.6*

Table C Relative productivity levels (whole economy 1986). Source: OECD

	GDP per head of population	GDP per person employed	GDP per hour worked
UK	100	100	100
US	150	141	132
Japan	106	94	67
Germany	110	113	105
France	106	119	117
Italy	100	–	–
Canada	140	131	116

Figures for Italy incomplete because of uncertainties in the size of the hidden economy.

Chapter Three
The balance of payments

'I never understood what those damned dots meant.' Lord
Randolph Churchill, Chancellor of the Exchequer (discussing statistics
presented in decimals)

Balance of payments accounts
A balance of payments is a summary of a country's international transactions over a given time period. Table 4 shows the UK balance of payments accounts over recent years, presented in two main sections: the
current account and **transactions** in UK assets and liabilities (which
was formerly known as the *capital account*). Table 5 shows the transactions in greater detail.

The difference between these two sections is essentially that the current account shows dealings in goods and services, while the transactions in UK assets and liabilities are short-term and long-term capital
movements. In a nutshell, international currency flows arising out of
consumption appear in the current account, while flows arising out of
investment appear in the assets and liabilities section. Generally speak-
ing, the assets and liabilities section tends to record 'once and for all'
expenditure (e.g. the building of a factory in the UK by a Japanese car
maker) while the current account is more likely to record 'recurring'
expenditures (e.g. the export of cars from that factory).

In both sections of Table 4, a positive amount indicates a flow of currency into the UK, and a minus sign (–) indicates a currency outflow.
Thus the sale of a British car to another country would show up as a
positive quantity in the current account. The building of an oil well in
the North Sea financed by a capital inflow from a Dutch oil company
would appear as a positive quantity in the assets and liabilities section.

Note that in Table 5 a minus sign indicates an *increase* in an external
asset and a *decrease* in an external liability.

Seasonal adjustment is necessary because of, for example, the effects
of the seasons on harvesting agricultural products, the closure of some
sea routes in winter, and the reduced rate of trade in the summer holidays. Seasonal adjustment uses an analysis of past data to remove dis-
tortions due to purely seasonal factors. An adjustment is also made to

Table 4 UK Balance of payments summary (£ million)

| | Seasonally adjusted | | | | | | Not seasonally adjusted | | | |
| | Visible trade (balance) | Invisibles (balances) | | | | Current balance | UK external assets and liabilities | | | Balancing item |
		Services	IPD*	transfers	Total		Transactions in assets	Transactions in liabilities	Net transactions	
1982	1 910	3 022	1 460	−1 741	2 741	4 649	−31 433	28 916	−2 519	−2 130
1983	−1 537	4 064	2 831	−1 593	5 302	3 765	−30 378	25 818	−4 562	797
1984	−5 336	4 519	4 357	−1 730	7 146	1 811	−31 918	24 153	−7 766	5 955
1985	−3 345	6 687	2 646	−3 111	6 222	2 878	−50 501	46 419	−4 082	1 204
1986	−9 559	6 808	5 096	−2 157	9 747	187	−92 663	85 430	−7 234	7 047
1987	−11 582	6 745	4 078	−3 400	7 423	−4 159	−79 627	85 438	5 810	−1 651
1988	−21 624	4 574	5 047	−3 518	6 103	−15 520	−55 426	65 071	9 645	5 875
1989	−24 598	4 685	4 088	−4 578	4 195	−20 404	−83 199	96 115	12 916	7 488
1990	−18 675	4 974	3 436	−4 935	3 475	−15 200	−72 399	87 035	14 636	564
1991 Q1	−2 988	1 234	−693	−241	300	−2 688	−9 762	13 627	3 865	−434
Q2	−2 104	1 748	90	139	1 977	−127	2 176	−9 452	−7 276	7 708
Q3	−2 345	1 520	518	−1 028	1 010	−1 335	−7 339	6 324	−1 015	3 167

* Interest (on portfolio assets such as bills and bonds), profits (from firms), and dividends (on shares).
Source: *Economic Trends*, December 1991.

Note: There are minor inconsistencies in some of the figures given in Tables 1, 2, 3 and 4. This is because balance of payments statistics are often inaccurate when first published and are later revised. This problem is further discussed in Chapter Seven.

Table 5 Summary of transactions in UK external assets and liabilities (£million, not seasonally adjusted)

| | Transactions in external assets | | | | | | Transactions in external liabilities | | | | | |
| | UK investment overseas | | Lending etc to overseas residents by UK banks | Deposits and lending overseas by UK residents other than banks and general government | Official reserves | Other external assets of central government | Overseas investment in the United Kingdom | | Borrowing etc from overseas residents by UK banks | Borrowing from overseas by UK residents other than banks and general government | Other external liabilities of general government | Net transactions |
	Direct	Portfolio					Direct	Portfolio				
1982	−4 091	−7 565	−20 566	−472	1 421	−161	3 027	−11	24 421	1 070	409	−2 519
1983	−5 417	−7 350	−18 443	702	607	−478	3 386	1 701	21 293	22	−584	−4 562
1984	−6 033	−9 759	−14 359	−1 932	908	−743	−181	1 288	24 790	−1 704	−40	−7 766
1985	−8 456	−16 755	−22 024	−777	−1 758	−730	3 865	9 671	29 443	3 416	24	−4 082
1986	−12 038	−22 095	−53 678	−1 453	−2 891	−509	4 987	11 785	64 127	4 353	178	−7 234
1987	−19 215	7 201	−50 427	−4 378	−12 012	−796	8 478	19 210	52 600	3 319	1 829	5 810
1988	−20 880	−8 600	−19 515	−2 779	−2 761	−891	10 236	14 387	34 218	5 399	831	9 645
1989	−21 521	−31 283	−27 032	−7 862	5 440	−942	17 145	13 239	43 887	19 658	2 186	12 916
1990	−8 913	−12 115	−37 477	−12 589	−79	−1 227	18 592	5 034	47 153	15 541	713	14 636
1991 Q1	−3 378	−7 637	4 256	−625	−2 147	−230	4 743	5 679	−2 186	6 412	−1 022	3 865
Q2	−3 084	−6 861	18 838	−5 683	−847	−188	3 076	5 630	−22 234	3 854	221	−7 276
Q3	−2 092	−7 707	5 043	−2 512	152	−223	1 754	3 487	−51	1 678	−543	−1 015

Source: *Economic Trends*, December 1991.

allow for the fact that months (and years) are of differing lengths. Movements in assets and liabilities are not so subject to marked seasonal changes, so no adjustment is made.

The current account

This account consists of two main sub-sections. The **visible trade** balance shows the difference between total spending on and income from visible items (i.e. goods). The visible trade balance is known as the *balance of trade*: a phrase often confused with the balance of payments as a whole. It is possible to identify and compare income from and expenditure on certain special categories of visible items which might be regarded as particularly important to the UK economy, such as 'manufactured goods' or basic commodities like oil. Statistics are often produced showing the balance of trade on manufactures, or comparing the 'oil' and 'non-oil' balances.

The **invisible balance** is the difference between spending on and income from invisible items (i.e. services, such as banking, insurance, transport and tourism).

Together the visible balance and the invisible balance give the **current balance**, which is the difference between spending on imports and income from exports of goods and services.

Transactions in external assets and liabilities

This section covers transactions made for investment, saving and borrowing purposes. These capital movements are undertaken by private individuals, firms and governments. For convenience we shall refer to these groups collectively as 'agents'. An **external asset** is something which agents in other countries must one day repay to agents in the UK – for example, the repayment of a loan which a French company borrows from a UK bank. If a UK bank lends money to a firm in France, then to begin with currency flows out of the UK so appears in the accounts as a *negative external asset*. When money is repaid the flow of currency from France to the UK would be recorded as a *positive external asset*.

On the other hand, an **external liability** refers to something which agents in the UK will one day have to repay to agents in other countries. So, if a firm in the UK borrows from a United States bank, then money flows into the UK and appears as a *positive external liability*. When money is repaid on the loan, however, the accounts will record a *negative external liability*.

In Table 5, **direct investment** refers to the purchase of real physical assets, such as a factory building. **Portfolio investment** refers to the buying and selling of securities, such as company shares. Together these will earn profit, interest and dividends (refer to the footnote of Table 4). Overseas investors will be encouraged to add to the flow of direct and portfolio investment funds into the UK if they have *confidence* in the future economic performance of the UK. A successful UK economy will create a market for the output of their direct investments, and generate the profits which will ensure an adequate return on their portfolio investments. 'Business confidence' is a difficult concept to pin down and it cannot be measured exactly, but good labour relations, buoyant levels of consumer spending, and a government which supports investment either through tax incentives or through direct financial assistance can all play a part in building it up. High levels of inflation, political instability and sudden changes in government policy, such as the 'stop-go' cycle (which is discussed in Chapter 8), can all harm business confidence.

Most items in the balance of payments accounts are known as autonomous transactions, which take place as a result of voluntary decisions by agents to buy, sell, lend or borrow. Changes in **official reserves** are an example of an **accommodating transaction**, which takes place in response to either a deficit or surplus in the overall balance of payments. if there is a surplus (so that currency inflows are greater than currency outflows) then official reserves are likely to show a positive entry, indicating that reserves of foreign currency have increased. A negative entry suggests that the monetary authorities have reduced their foreign currency reserves to help finance a deficit (outflows being greater than inflows). Note that the changes in official reserves might not exactly match the balance of payments deficit, since the authorities might seek to meet some of the shortage of foreign currency created by the deficit through borrowing. The Bank of England, on behalf of the government, could borrow from the central banks of other countries, or from the International Monetary Fund (see Chapter 4). Such borrowings, creating a currency inflow, would register as a positive item, while the repayment of overseas debt would carry a negative sign.

While most capital movements are relatively *long-term* in nature, some of the items in the assets and liabilities section correspond to *short-term* monetary movements between countries. In recent years, with the deregulation of money markets and the abolition of exchange controls, governments have become more sensitive to flows of **hot money**. These flows of capital between the financial centres of the world can have harmful effects, especially when a 'run' on a particular currency causes a loss of confidence which can lead to a collapse in a currency's stability. However, under some circumstances, short-term flows of capital can support a currency which would otherwise be in difficulty. In the mid-

1980s, for instance, the UK balance of payments moved into a large deficit, but it was not until 1989 that the government had to draw upon its foreign currency reserves. This was largely due to the fact that interest rates were much higher in the UK than in many other countries, particularly the United States, so this encouraged financiers in other countries to place their deposits in UK financial institutions.

Balancing item

The balance of payments figures are put together from a number of different sources, and the degree of accuracy varies considerably. They often have to be revised after they have first been published, when previously unrecorded items come to light. Capital flows have become more difficult to keep track of with the abolition of exchange controls and the deregulation of financial markets.

In principle the overall balance of payments should balance by summing to zero. This is in line with what is called 'double entry bookkeeping'. This is because, in theory, every balance of payments transaction should involve equal credit and debit entries. For instance, the export of a machine from the UK to France would appear as a positive item in the current account, because payment for the machine will flow into the UK and be deposited in a UK bank. Elsewhere in the accounts this transaction is likely to be matched by a negative item, for instance if the French importer has acquired sterling from a UK financial institution in order to purchase the machine.

However, information on the two entries made in respect of each transaction generally comes from at least two different sources, and there is scope for inaccuracies. There might, for instance, be time delays causing the two entries to appear in accounts for different time periods; they might be converted into sterling at different exchange rates; or it might be that the sophistication of accounting and recording procedures might differ from country to country. In order to bring the total of all entries to zero, the **balancing item** is included to reflect human error and unspecified items in compiling the accounts. The large size of the balancing item in recent years has cast doubt on the accuracy of balance of payments figures, particularly at the immediate time of publication, and in March 1990 the then Chancellor of the Exchequer, Nigel Lawson, ordered a radical review of the way in which balance of payments statistics are collected.

Equilibrium

Since in *accounting* terms the balance of payments must always balance, how can the balance of payments be a problem? It can be a problem in *economic* terms because a balance of payments surplus means that the net demand for sterling over a given time period is greater than the supply; while the opposite is true for a deficit. With a *floating* exchange rate (see Chapter 4), demand and supply can be brought into **equilibrium** with an alteration in the exchange rate. With fixed exchange rates the central authority must bring demand and supply into equilibrium by buying or selling sterling. As we shall see, it is possible to argue that a deficit in the balance of payments is not necessarily bad, while a surplus is not necessarily good. For example, a deficit can be regarded as a form of short-term borrowing, to increase future growth. A deficit might be a sign that a country is purchasing raw materials to be turned into goods for a future export drive. The deficit becomes a problem when it is persistent in the long term, and foreign currency reserves are insufficient to finance it. Therefore, although the balance of payments must always balance, as an accountant's balance sheet, there is a problem in *performing the balancing act* through economic policy.

A surplus, on the other hand, might not necessarily indicate that a country has a generally successful economy. It could be argued, for instance, that the UK's oil surpluses have served to disguise basic weaknesses in the UK economy, and by keeping the rate of exchange of sterling higher than it would otherwise have been, have actually made UK exports even less competitive. Also, it could be argued that one country's surplus is another country's deficit, and that it is in nobody's long-term interests for one country (or group of countries such as OPEC) to have persistent surpluses, thus impoverishing their trading partners to the future detriment of world trade as a whole. Modern thinking tends to favour the concept of 'equilibrium' in the balance of payments. While it would be a statistical miracle for every country in the world to find that its exports exactly match its imports, and it would be logically impossible for every country in the world to have a huge surplus, modern thinking has moved on from the days of the *Mercantilists* when all that mattered was the trade of the mother country. Today, most economists would probably argue that in an ideal world there would be a general expansion of trade and living standards together with countries aiming at balance of payments equilibrium – defined to mean that over a period of years, deficits and surpluses tend to cancel each other out. In the subject of economics, beware of emotive words which can mislead – see the boxed item 'For whom the gloom tolls'.

UK deficits

It is important to note that *financing* a deficit is not the same thing as *curing* a deficit. Deficits can be financed by using foreign currency

For whom the gloom tolls

Beware emotive words linked to economic indicators

It is bound to end in tears: some economists are trying to give their dismal science sex appeal. To make dry numbers more alluring, economic and financial commentators add emotive adjectives or nouns: gloom, worsening, cheer, improved. But the next time you spot the word gloom in a headline or read that a trade balance has deteriorated, ask this question: gloom for whom? The answer may be surprisingly cheery.

Commentators should mind their tongues when it comes to trade. America's trade balance is said to "improve" as its deficit shrinks, Germany's to "deteriorate" as its surplus disappears. Yet a trade surplus is a misleading measure of a country's economic strength, or a deficit of its weakness. Barring further information, it is neutral. The recent disappearance of Germany's surplus is to be welcomed: to the extent that the surge in domestic demand after reunification has been met by imports, it has helped to check inflation. And is a rise in Japan's trade surplus an improvement or a deterioration? It provokes protectionism and means Japanese consumers are not enjoying as many imports as they might – but it also means that Japan is transferring its savings to the rest of the world.

The idea that surpluses are good and deficits bad comes from the nasty mercantilist view that exports are good and imports are bad: yet the only reason to export is to enable your consumers to buy lots of luvverly imports. For as long as foreigners were willing to finance the American deficit, Americans enjoyed a higher standard of living than they otherwise would have. When Mexico was in a debt-ridden mess, its current-account deficits were "bad" because they could be financed only with short-term borrowing. Now that it has lowered trade barriers and opened its economy to foreign investment, its current-account deficit is a sign of strength: imports of capital goods and others are being financed by foreign direct investment. Economic commentators take note. Trade surpluses and deficits increase, rise, grow, widen or swell, but they never improve.

Source: Adapted from *The Economist*, 31 August 1991

reserves, by borrowing from the IMF or the central banks of other countries, or by increasing domestic interest rates. High rates of interest can seriously damage the domestic economy, while reserves cannot be run down indefinitely. Policies for tackling as opposed to financing a deficit will be discussed in Chapters 8 and 9. For the time being, suffice

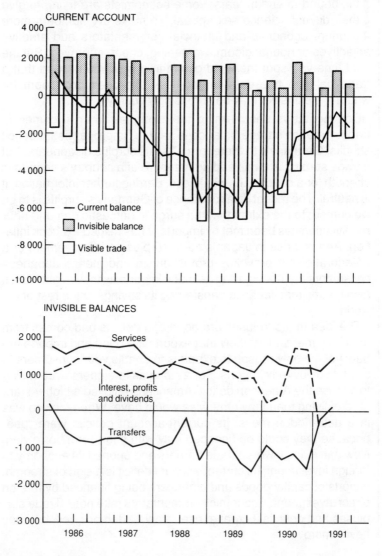

Figure 5 UK balance of payments (£million). Source *Economic Trends*, December 1991

it to say that short-term currency inflows can be a sign that agents overseas are supplying the UK with currency which it is failing to earn from its current account transactions. For this reason, economic analysts tend to focus their attentions on the balance of visibles and invisibles, since these figures are felt to indicate the extent to which the UK's day-to-day transactions are paying their way. If we wish to explore the theme of 'UK plc' we must therefore focus on the current account, and this will be the main focus of attention in the rest of this book.

Figure 5 traces the performance of the current account in recent years. The UK traditionally has a visible trade deficit, which means that the country spends more money buying goods and commodities from abroad than we earn from selling foods and commodities to other countries. If there were no trade in services, then the country would continually run into debt. The top graph shows that between 1986 and 1987 the visible deficit increased while the invisible balance decreased, so that the overall current account went into deficit. The deficit hit record levels in the late 1980s, and still had not achieved a balance by 1992.

KEY WORDS

Current account	Direct investment
Transactions	Portfolio investment
Seasonal adjustment	Autonomous transactions
Visible trade	Official reserves
Invisible balance	Accommodating transaction
Current balance	Hot money
External asset	Balancing item
External liability	Equilibrium

Reading list

Central Statistical Office, UK Balance of Payments (The Pink Book), HMSO.

Paisley, R. and Quillfeldt, J., Exercises 5 and 8 in *Economics Investigated*, Collins Educational, 1989.

Essay topics

1. What has been the contribution of 'invisibles' to the balance of payments on current account in the past decade? Account for the changes that occurred in invisibles. (Oxford & Cambridge Schools Examination Board, 1991)

2. Outline the main trends in Britain's foreign trade in recent decades and indicate their possible causes. Discuss whether or not a deficit on current account is a sign of strength or weakness in Britain's economic performance. (Joint Matriculation Board, 1989)

Data Response Question 3

Balance of payments figures

This task is based on a question set by the University of London School Examinations Board in 1991. Study Table A, in which the data relate to the net sums (credits less debits) of various items in the balance of payments of the United Kingdom since 1980, and answer the questions.

Table A Some balance of payments figures (£ million)

	1980	1982	1984	1986	1988
Visible balance	1 355	1 908	–5 169	–9 364	–20 826
Invisibles					
Services					
Government	–850	–1 350	–1 181	–1 400	–1 833
Travel	223	-452	–49	–530	–2 042
Financial services	3 883	4 911	5 926	9 062	9 478
Other services	397	–138	–357	–885	–1 438
Interest, profits and dividends	–204	1 449	4 449	5 364	5 619
Transfers	–1 984	–1 741	–1 734	–2 181	–3 575

Source: *United Kingdom Balance of Payments*, 1989, HMSO

1. Identify one of the expenditures which is included in each of the following items: (i) government; (ii) transfers.
2. Compare the contributions made by the balance of all invisible items to the UK's current account balance in 1980 and 1988.
3. Account for the changes in the net receipts from the following items during the period shown: (i) travel; (ii) financial services; (iii) interest, profits and dividends.
4. Examine the factors which might explain the change in the net visible balance during the period shown.

Chapter Four
Trade and exchange rates

'The European Monetary System provides many pointers for the future of the international monetary system ... But the regional option only makes sense eventually in the context of a reformed monetary system in the whole world.' The Brandt Commission

Trade and exchange rates

The **exchange rate** is the rate at which national currencies are exchanged – for example pounds and dollars, pounds and deutschmarks or dollars and deutschmarks.

We have seen that specialization necessitates trade. It is also the case that international trade has necessitated the creation of an international monetary system. You are probably used to seeing imported American programmes on the television in the UK. Have you ever stopped to consider how such things are paid for? If a UK television company purchases an episode of 'Cheers' from Hollywood, then the production company in the USA will not wish to be paid in pounds sterling. Pounds cannot be spent in California, and so it will require payment in dollars. This means that someone in the UK television organization will have to acquire dollars from a bank. In effect this means that pounds are offered on the foreign exchange market in order to acquire dollars. If, on the other hand, a UK television company exports the 'Inspector Morse' series to the USA,

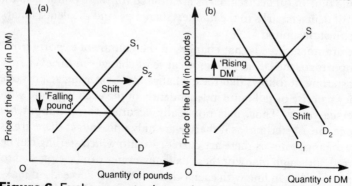

Figure 6 Exchange rate determination: falling pound

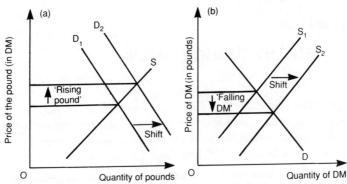

Figure 7 Exchange rate determination: rising pound

then the American television companies will need to purchase pounds in order to pay for it.

Similarly, trade between the UK and Germany will affect the demand for and supply of pounds and deutschmarks. This can be illustrated in two ways: we can either visualize the process as a change in the supply of pounds, or a change in the demand for deutschmarks. In Figure 6 the shift of the supply curve in diagram (a) along with the shift in the demand curve in diagram (b) show the effect on the foreign exchange market of an import from Germany into the UK. The effect of an increase in imports, other things being equal, is therefore to reduce the exchange rate of the pound (when measured in deutschmarks), as in (a); and to increase the exchange rate of the DM (measured in pounds), as in (b).

We can visualize the effect of an export from the UK to Germany as in Figure 7(a), where the demand for pounds on the foreign exchange markets increases, and the pound rises against the deutschmark; and at the same time in (b) deutschmarks are offered for these pounds, so the supply of deutschmarks to the markets increases, and the deutschmark falls against the pound.

The argument here is that changes in the volume of exports from, and imports to, the UK are a major cause of changes in the exchange rate of sterling. It follows that the exchange rate of sterling against one currency can rise or fall quite independently of the exchange rate with another currency. Thus, it is not really accurate to talk about *the* exchange rate of sterling, as if there were only one. In fact there are as many exchange rates as there are currencies into which sterling can be converted, although many of these exchange rates can be expected to move more or less in line with each other – if the UK succeeds in making its exports more attractive to one trading partner, they are likely to become more attractive to other countries also; and many currencies, such as those belonging to the Exchange Rate Mechanism (ERM) of the EC, are becoming increasingly harmonized. Even so, if we are asked whether the pound is 'rising' or 'falling' then the question only really makes sense if another currency is mentioned against which we can plot the pound's movements. Often economists use a 'basket of currencies' to gain as general a picture as possible of the pound's movements.

Apart from the volume of trade, other influences on the exchange rate of sterling include inflation, interest rates, speculation, and government policy.

Inflation

If the inflation rate in the UK is higher than that in other countries, then British exports become less attractive to customers in other countries, and cheaper imports become more attractive to British customers. Inflation thus tends to cause imports to rise faster than exports. It reduces any surplus in the balance of payments, or increases any deficit, and thus tends to reduce the exchange rate of the pound. Economists sometimes use a concept known as *purchasing power parity* to allow for different cost-of-living levels in different countries. This is discussed later.

Interest rates

A rise in UK interest rates encourages people and institutions in other countries to deposit money with UK financial institutions. This will, in effect, create a demand for pounds and increase the exchange rate of sterling against the currency of the country which is the source of such funds. The government of the UK can to some extent influence the value of the pound on foreign exchange markets by manipulating UK interest rates upwards and downwards, thus influencing the flow of financial deposits between the UK and other countries. We mentioned these flows as 'hot money' in Chapter 3.

Speculation

It would be grossly misleading to suggest that all dealings in foreign exchange arise from transactions in exports and imports. Around 90 per cent of transactions, by value, are from speculation. This is the buying and selling of currency not to finance trade, but in order to 'gamble' on future trends on the market. Speculators aim to purchase currencies at one price and sell them at a higher price, or gain high interest rates.

A certain amount of speculation can be seen to be useful, since it ensures that there is always an availability of a very wide range of currencies, and it virtually guarantees that it is always possible to sell currencies; no matter how unattractive a certain currency might appear, some speculator will buy it if the price is right. However, excessive speculation can be severely criticized: flows of 'hot' money constantly seeking quick profits can harm confidence and lead to instability, which makes long-term economic development very difficult, and a 'run' on a currency being caused by rumour and innuendo is a possibility. This loss of confidence in a currency can become a self-fulfilling prophecy, causing a currency to collapse for reasons which are only loosely connected with a country's true trading position.

Government policy

At times, government policy can affect exchange rates. This might happen in a general and imprecise way, with the success or otherwise of economic policy contributing towards an atmosphere of confidence or gloom which might affect the exchange rate. Or it might happen in a deliberate and direct way, with the government – through its central bank – using its reserves to purchase the domestic currency, or building up its reserves while selling the domestic currency, in order to influence its exchange rate upwards or downwards. If the Bank of England enters the foreign exchange market to buy sterling when its price is falling, then the evening news headline will be *'The Bank supports sterling'*.

Effects of changes in an exchange rate

As we shall see in Chapter 5, exchange rates have at various times been fixed or floating. **Fixed exchange rates** are 'managed' by governments, and any adjustments are made deliberately by the government or its monetary authorities. **Floating exchange rates** are allowed to find their own level according to the 'laws' of supply and demand; and there are various methods of 'dirty floating' where market forces are allowed to operate, but where the government intervenes from time to time.

There are occasions when a government might wish to *revalue* its currency or see it *appreciate* so that its exchange value rises against other currencies. At other times the government might wish the currency to *devalue* or *depreciate* – that is, to reduce its exchange value. (The terms **revaluation** and **devaluation** are usually used to signify a change in exchange rate brought about by deliberate government action, whereas use of the terms **appreciation** or **depreciation** usually suggests that a change in exchange rates has occurred as a result of an 'automatic' adjustment, with the forces of supply and demand allowing exchange rates to 'float' to their own level.)

We saw above that it is wrong to speak of 'the' exchange rate as if there were only one, because when exchange rates float it is possible for a currency to be appreciating against some currencies and depreciating against others. For this reason statisticians have attempted to define an **effective exchange rate**, such as a **trade weighted index**, which attempts to show the value of sterling measured against a 'basket of currencies' which averages sterling's movements against the currencies of its major trading partners. It is also possible to attempt to calculate a **real exchange rate** (as opposed to a **nominal exchange rate**), which takes into account differences in international inflation rates.

Purchasing power parity is a theory which suggests that the exchange rate between two currencies will ultimately reflect their domestic purchasing powers. For instance, if it costs £1 to buy a certain basket of goods in the UK, and $2 to buy the same basket in the USA, then the exchange rate is likely to be £1 = $2. While purchasing power parities can be useful in indicating the extent to which inflation can affect the international competitiveness of trading nations, domestic prices are not the only influence on exchange rates. Different countries have different consumption patterns, and therefore it is very difficult to choose a 'typical' basket of goods. Some goods are only consumed at home and hardly figure in international trade at all. There are some goods which have become global in their nature, and the *Economist*

The hamburger standard

The Economist newspaper's correspondents check the price of a Big Mac every three years. Why a Big Mac? It is internationally a homogeneous product, produced locally (even in Moscow), so there will be no distorting distribution costs.

The Big Mac standard is the US price in dollars. The purchasing power parity (PPP) for the dollar is then calculated as the foreign price divided by the dollar price. Below are some selected examples from its 1989 table.

Currency	Local price	Dollar PPP	Actual exchange rate	Percentage- under-valuation of dollar
Britain	£1.26	0.62	0.59	5
Japan	Y370	183	133	27
Germany	DM4.30	2.13	1.89	11

Exercise: These 1989 figures are now out of date, so update them for Britain today. Your local Big Mac price? Sterling's spot price yesterday? Assume that the Big Mac now costs, say, $2.10 in the USA.

magazine has found that the prices of Macdonalds' hamburgers can be used as a basis for an index which works quite accurately in predicting rates of exchange.

It has been mentioned above that a number of factors can influence exchange rates. However, it is undeniably true that a major cause of balance of payments disequilibria might well be uncompetitiveness due to inflation, which puts domestic prices out of line with prices internationally, and so purchasing power parities clearly have some long-term influence on exchange rates.

In recent years, as a country with persistent deficits on the balance of payments, the UK has often experienced a downward pressure on sterling. It is therefore pertinent to examine some of the possible effects of devaluation.

Suppose a firm in the UK is selling cars to a showroom in Switzerland. The price of the car in the UK is £10 000. If the exchange rate is £1 = 3 Swiss francs, then a Swiss importer will need to pay 30 000 francs in order to purchase the car. Now suppose the pound depreciates, or is devalued, so that £1 = 2 Swiss francs. Now a Swiss importer needs to offer only 20 000 francs in order to buy the same car. Thus, a depreciation of the domestic currency makes a country's exports cheaper; it also has the effect of making imports more expensive to buy. Does this necessarily mean that a depreciation of the currency will improve a country's balance of payments?

The Marshall-Lerner condition

This principle states that for a depreciation of a currency to improve a country's balance of trade, then the price elasticity of demand for a country's exports, plus the price elasticity of demand for its imports, must be greater than unity: in other words the total demand for a country's exports and imports must be price elastic. The idea underlying this principle is the one which has been discussed above: that a depreciation effectively causes an increase in the price of imports and a decrease in the price of imports. It can thus be predicted that, in terms of volume, the balance of trade will improve. However, in terms of revenues and costs (i.e. prices times volume), it is only if the elasticity of exports plus the elasticity of imports is greater than one that the improvement in the revenue from exports is enough to offset the increased cost of imports. In Figure 8, can you find *eleven* cases where devaluation can be successful? The 'classic' case is perhaps the best one, being the easiest to understand. (This is the last one illustrated.)

While the Marshall-Lerner condition might be an important condition for a successful devaluation, there are other conditions which might be equally or more important. For example, devaluation could fail because of problems on the supply side of the economy: if, for instance, domestic producers had insufficient spare capacity, then they might have a very inelastic supply curve so that they could not respond to an increased demand for their products with higher output.

Is devaluation inflationary?

We have used the phrase 'successful devaluation' above. By 'successful' is meant successful in relation to tackling a balance of payments deficit. Even if this is achieved, a devaluation might well be a 'failure' in broader terms if it causes other problems in the economy. For example, standard textbooks assert that a falling exchange rate leads to higher inflation, through higher priced imports and, therefore, trade union pressure for higher wage growth. During the 1980s, however, there was little empirical evidence to link falls in the pound with the unleashing of a wage/price spiral. Because of high unemployment and the absence of incomes policies, the levels of sterling and average earnings moved more or less independently of each other. On the other hand, by making imported raw materials more expensive, devaluation might still contribute to 'cost push' inflation to some extent. It depends on whether importers absorb some, or all, of the expected price rise as lower profits instead, in order to protect their market shares.

It should not be assumed that, given the correct conditions, all that needs to be done to 'cure' a balance of payments problem is to devalue. In the long sweep of economic history this might well turn out to be a 'temporary' solution. In later chapters we examine some of the longer-term trends in UK trade: longer term trends might well require longer-term policies.

The J-curve effect

Figure 9 refers to another possible effect of devaluation. In response to a balance of payments deficit, the government devalues the currency. This affects the price of imports (their prices rise from the point of view of the domestic consumer). It also affects the price of exports (their prices rise, from the point of view of the overseas consumer). If imported raw materials are needed to produce more exports, the deficit might worsen in the short run before it improves in the long run. Hence the J shape of the curve.

- Why is it important to distinguish between the *volume* and the *value* of exports and imports?
- How is the J-curve related to the Marshall–Lerner condition?

ED combinations		ΣED	Balance of trade effect*	EXPORTS		
Exports	Imports			ED	Export earnings (£ value)	Cases
A (0)	A (1)	1	K	0	SAME	
A (0)	B (>0 <1)	<1	↓			
A (0)	C (0)	<1	↓			
A (0)	D (>1)	>1	↑	>0 <1	HIGHER (slightly)	
B (>0 <1)	A (1)	>1	↑			
B (>0 <1)	B (>0 <1)	1	K	1	HIGHER (much)	
B (>0 <1)	B (>0 <1)	>1	↑			
B (>0 <1)	B (>0 <1)	<1	↓			
B (>0 <1)	C (0)	<1	↓	>1	HIGHER (very much)	
B (>0 <1)	D (>1)	>1	↑			

Cases (Foreign exchange price vs Q):
- A: D, ED=0, Constant Q × constant Sterling price
- B: ED = $\frac{1}{4}$, >Q × constant £ price
- C: ED = 1, > Q × constant £ price
- D: ED = >1, > Q × constant £ price

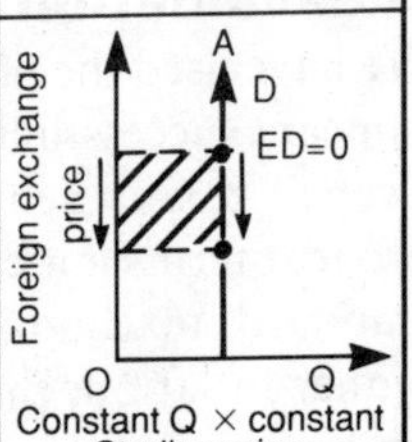

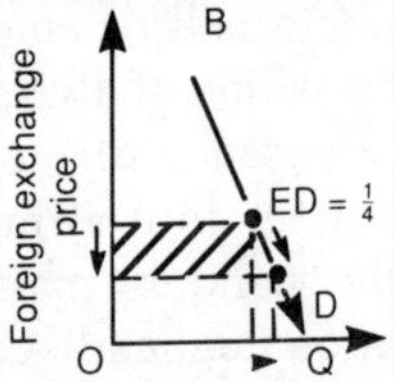

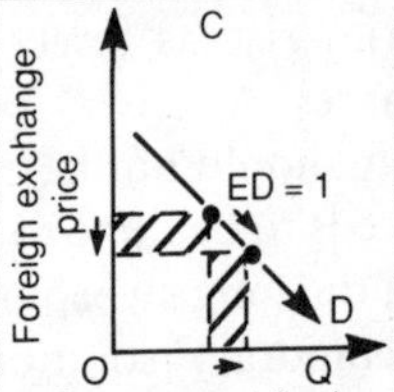

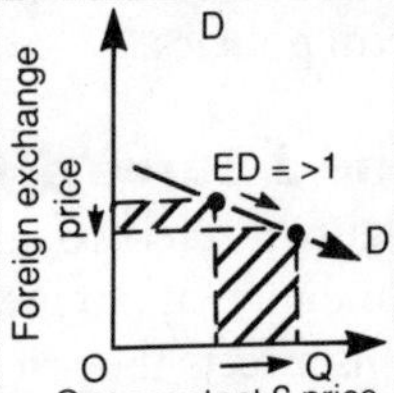

K = constant
↓ = deterioration
↑ = improvement

Figure 8 Elasticities of demand (*ED*) for exports and imports following devaluation: assumptions of constant sterling prices of exports and constant foreign

IMPORTS			ED combinations		ΣED	Balance of trade effect
Cases	Import bill (£ value)	ED	Exports	Imports		
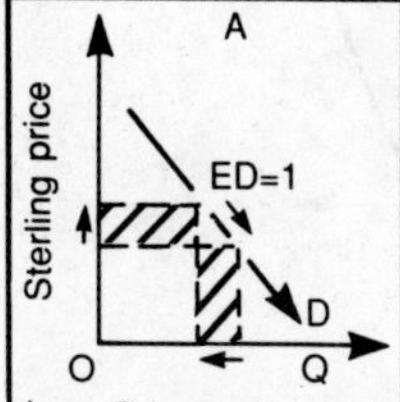 Less Q×>sterling price	SAME	1	C (1)	A (1)	>1	↑
			C (1)	B (>0 <1)	>1	↑
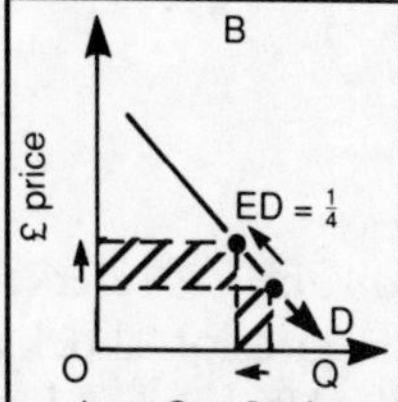 Less Q×>£ price	HIGHER (slightly)	>0 <1	C (1)	C (0)	1	K
			C (1)	D (>1)	>1	↑
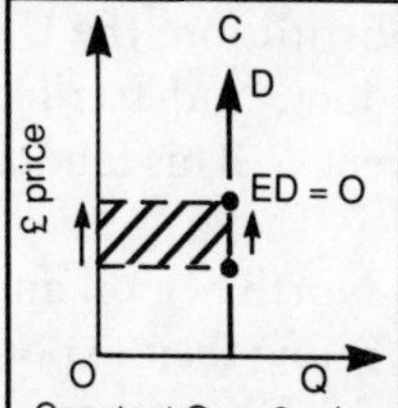 Constant Q×> £ price	HIGHER (much)	0	D (>1)	A (1)	>1	↑
			D (>1)	B (>0 <1)	>1	↑
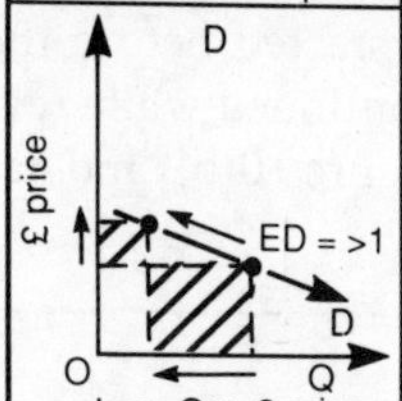 Less Q×>£ price	LOWER	>1	D (>1)	C (0)	>1	↑
			D (>1)	D (>1)	>1	↑

exchange prices of imports. Source *Comprehensive Economics* by B.V. Marshall (Longman)

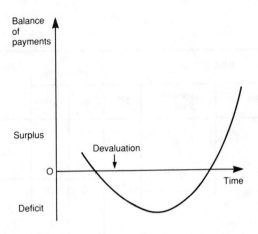

Figure 9 The J-curve

North Sea oil and gas

Figure 10 indicates the effect of the UK's North Sea oil and gas reserves on sterling. While the world economy has suffered a series of 'shocks' from changes in the price of energy (Figure 10(a)), the UK has become self-sufficient in oil. This has resulted in import substitution; the UK has become an exporter of a major primary product, and sterling became in the early 1980s, for a while, a 'petrocurrency'. This tended to 'buoy up' its price.

Sterling in 1980 and 1981 was over-valued. This North Sea oil and gas damaged other sectors of the UK economy by harming their export competitiveness. The decline in manufacturing in the UK cannot be entirely explained in this way, however, since it started before the development of the North Sea oilfields, and has continued while revenue from North Sea production peaked in 1986 (Figure 10(b)) and has since declined.

KEY WORDS

Exchange rate	Effective exchange rate
Fixed exchange rates	Trade weighted index
Floating exchange rates	Real exchange rate
Revaluation	Nominal exchange rate
Devaluation	Purchasing power parity
Appreciation	Marshall-Lerner condition
Depreciation	J-curve effect

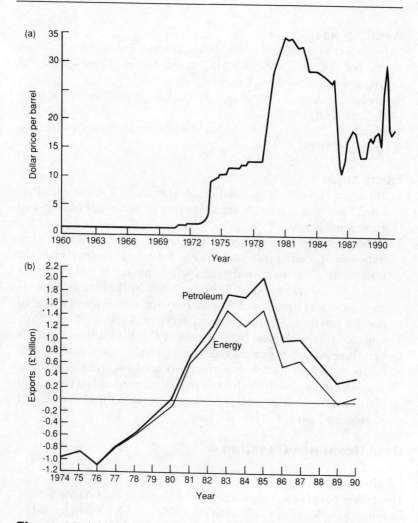

Figure 10 (a) World oil price, and (b) UK petroleum and energy net exports. Source *UK Balance of Payments 1991*

Reading list

Independent Commission on International Development Issues (chaired by Willy Brandt), Chapter 13 in *North–South: A Programme for Survival*, Pan, 1981.

Samuelson, P.A. and Nordhaus, W.D., Chapter 40 in *Economics*, McGraw-Hill, 1989.

Stanlake, G., Chapter 18 in *Macroeconomics: An Introduction*, Longman, 1989.

Essay topics

1. What are the advantages and disadvantages of a stable exchange rate? How might a stable exchange rate be achieved? (Associated Examining Board, 1990)

2. 'In an increasingly integrated world, the exchange rate is both a key indicator of economic conditions and a most important part of the transmission mechanism through which monetary policy affects inflation'. (Nigel Lawson, 1989). Explain why the exchange rate is an indicator of the state of the economy and how it may be used to control inflation. (Joint Matriculation Board, 1990)

3. One advantage claimed for a system of flexible exchange rates is that there is a self-regulating mechanism which automatically solves balance of payments deficits without any need for government intervention. (a) Explain how this self-regulating mechanism works. (b) What factors might prevent this system from operating? (Associated Examining Board, 1991)

Data Response Question 4

Purchasing power parity

This task is based on a question set by the University of London School Examinations Board in 1991. Read the article, which is taken from *The Financial Times* of 10 February 1987, and answer the following questions.

1. What do you understand by purchasing power parity?
2. Why might exchange rates not reflect purchasing power parities?
3. Explain the meaning of the statement: 'In nominal terms some countries, especially Japan, have recently moved much closer to the US.'
4. '... per capita GDP in nominal terms rose to $16 200 in Japan in 1986 compared with $10 997 in 1985, reflecting the appreciation of the yen against the dollar.' Discuss the implications of this statement.

Living standards in the US continue to be well above those of other Western countries according to the latest calculations on purchasing power parities (PPPs) by the OECD.

The OECD calculations show the only country approaching the US living standards is Canada whose real per capita gross domestic product is about 90% of the US figure.

In nominal terms some countries, especially Japan, have recently moved much closer to the US. But the narrowing of the gap essentially reflects the increase in the exchange rate converted dollar prices in these countries. The quantities of goods and services per capita in Japan remain at about 30% below the US level.

GDP per capita in the US rose from $16 494 in 1985 to $17 200 in 1986. By comparison, Canadian GDP per capita rose on the PPPs basis from $14 959 in 1985 to $15 700 in 1986. In Japan, the figures were $11 666 and $12 200 respectively. But converted at exchange rates rather than using PPPs, per capita GDP in nominal terms rose to $16 200 in Japan in 1986 compared with $10 997 in 1985, reflecting the appreciation of the yen against the dollar.

Chapter Five
Sterling's place in the world

'Down, down, down. Would the fall never come to an end?' Lewis
Carroll, Alice in Wonderland

The sterling exchange rate
Table 6 shows how the sterling exchange rate has fluctuated in recent
years against the Japanese yen, the American dollar, Swiss franc,
French franc, Italian lira and the German deutschmark.

By maintaining reserves of foreign currencies the government can,
through the Bank of England, intervene in the foreign exchange markets to buy and sell sterling. Purchasing sterling (selling foreign currencies) increases the demand for pounds and hence tends to push its price
up; selling sterling (purchasing foreign currencies) increases the supply
of pounds and thus helps to keep its price down. Refer again to Figures
6 and 7 to visualize this process in action.

General problems of international trade and payments
The world system of international payments has always had to overcome three problems: liquidity, adjustment, and confidence.

The liquidity problem
Because it is a fairly rare metal, gold has always been acceptable as a
form of international currency. Indeed, for many years (before 1914 and
from 1925 to 1931) many countries including the UK were on the **gold
standard**, whereby their currencies were fixed by law in terms of gold. A
serious problem with gold is that its supply is virtually limited to the output of the gold mines of South Africa and the Commonwealth of
Independent States (formerly the Soviet Union). Relying on these countries to underpin world trade would clearly cause tremendous political
problems; and even if their political systems had altered much more
quickly than they have, the output of gold would have been insufficient
to finance the tremendous expansion of international trade since the
Second World War. As well as gold, therefore, **reserve currencies** have
been established; and because of their dominance of the immediate post-

Table 6 Sterling exchange rates and UK official reserves (not seasonally adjusted)

	Sterling exchange rate against major currencies*						UK official reserves at end of period ($ million)†	Sterling exchange rate index (average 1985 = 100)
	Japanese yen	US dollar	Swiss franc	French franc	Italian lira	Deutschmark		
1983	359.89	1.5158	3.1820	11.5469	2 302	3.870	17 817	105.3
1984	316.80	1.3364	3.1291	11.6365	2 339	3.790	15 694	100.6
1985	307.08	1.2976	3.1550	11.5495	2 463	3.784	15 543	100.0
1986	246.80	1.4672	2.6350	10.1569	2 186	3.183	21 923	91.5
1987	236.50	1.6392	2.4394	9.8369	2 123	2.941	44 326	90.1
1988	227.98	1.7796	2.6030	10.5969	2 315	3.124	51 685	95.5
1989	225.66	1.6383	2.6780	10.4476	2 247	3.079	38 645	92.6
1990	257.38	1.7864	2.4687	9.6891	2 133	2.876	38 464	91.3
1991 Jan	258.60	1.9348	2.4593	9.9181	2 195	2.920	38 368	94.1
Feb	256.33	1.9657	2.4917	9.9019	2 183	2.909	41 794	94.3
Mar	250.44	1.8242	2.5324	9.9859	2 189	2.934	42 258	92.9
Apr	239.68	1.7480	2.5183	10.0630	2 207	2.979	43 591	92.3
May	238.00	1.7220	2.5105	10.0453	2 199	2.964	43 711	9.7
Jun	230.37	1.6510	2.5223	9.9775	2 186	2.941	44 264	90.2
Jul	227.65	1.6526	2.5559	10.0072	2 196	2.948	44 631	90.4
Aug	230.23	1.6828	2.5616	9.9748	2 194	2.935	44 691	90.7
Sep	231.68	1.7228	2.5588	9.9556	2 186	2.925	44 593	91.0
Oct	224.95	1.7227	2.5474	9.9253	...	2.911	44 252	90.5
Nov	...	...	...	...	...	...	43 915	...

*Average of daily telegraphic transfer rates in London; †Apart from transactions, the level of official reserves is affected by changes in the dollar valuation of gold, Special Drawing Rights and convertible currencies.
Source: *Economic Trends*, December 1991

war scene, the dollar and sterling – being the currencies of the USA and the UK – became established as major reserve currencies. A reserve currency is one which countries and international organizations are willing to hold in their foreign exchange reserves and which is used to finance international trade. The major reserve currencies are now the dollar and deutschmark; sterling has declined greatly in recent years.

Until the late 1950s, the US dollar was the currency in heaviest demand, although because of its historical links with the British Empire (now known as the Commonwealth, but not to be confused with the Commonwealth of Independent States) sterling also played a role as a reserve currency. In 1940 the term **Sterling Area** was officially coined to describe a group of countries, based mainly on the countries of the Commonwealth, using sterling as a medium of exchange for international trade, and holding reserves in the form of sterling balances in London. Up until 1939 sterling was freely convertible into other currencies. **Exchange control** was introduced at the outbreak of the Second World War, limiting its convertibility, but maintaining the free circulation of sterling within the Sterling Area. During the 1970s, following the oil price crisis, the move towards floating exchange rates and the abolition of exchange controls in 1978, sterling no longer carried a special status. Other **hard currencies** (currencies for which demand is high relative to supply), such as the yen and the deutschmark, were used instead.

World trade has grown faster than the gold and currency reserves of the trading countries. Attempts have therefore been made to create artificial international currencies: notably the *Special Drawing Rights* (SDRs) of the International Monetary Fund (IMF), and the *European Currency Unit* (ECU).

The confidence problem

Dealers who work on the currency exchange markets of the world are indispensable to those who wish to convert currencies, but there are times when the speculative side of their dealings can contribute to a crisis of **confidence** in the international monetary system.

In principle, exchange rates are determined by the necessity to change currencies in order to pay for exports and imports. In practice, large purchases of currencies are made by **speculators,** who deal on foreign exchange markets in order to purchase currencies at one price and sell at a higher price. Thus the major proportion of dealing in foreign exchange is speculative, rather than intended to finance trade.

Speculators can cause instability, through causing a run on a currency. If speculators *think* that a currency is about to collapse, then this can become a self-fulfilling prophecy as they rush to convert this currency into another and thereby *cause* a crash.

It is particularly important that there should be confidence in the reserve currencies. Past strains in the international monetary system have been especially acute when the USA and the UK have sought to overcome balance of payments deficits through devaluation. In the 1960s, for instance, when sterling was still very much a reserve currency, devaluation was described in terms of being a 'crisis'; the then Prime Minister, Harold Wilson, described it as 'a disaster, a dishonour, a disgrace' (he devalued in 1967). During the early 1980s, however, when sterling had lost this reserve status and had yet to be put into the ERM, its value could float down (and up) against other currencies without the Prime Minister having to appear on television to address the nation. If the proposals for a European common currency are to come to anything, an important prerequisite will be that people and institutions will be prepared to accept it in exchange for goods, keep their life savings in it, and allow it to perform all the other tasks expected of a currency in which they are confident.

The adjustment problem

Under the rules of the **Bretton Woods** agreement of 1945, a system of **fixed exchange rates** was set up whereby currencies were *pegged* at a 'par value' in relation to the US dollar, and allowed to fluctuate to a limit of 1 per cent either side of parity. The dollar itself was pegged to gold at a fixed price. In theory, a country with a persistent surplus would revalue upwards, while a deficit country would devalue. In practice, countries like West Germany with surpluses year after year saw little incentive to revalue, while the experience of the UK, a country which more often than not found itself in deficit, was that devaluation came to be seen as a political disaster, something which could only be done as an admission of defeat and in an atmosphere of crisis.

During the 1960s many people believed that the UK's main economic problems could be solved automatically by a system of **floating exchange rates**, whereby they would find their own level following the laws of supply and demand. In June 1972, sterling was floated on a 'temporary' basis – which in the event lasted until September 1990 when the pound was put into the European exchange rate mechanism. Sterling is now part of two distinct systems, both fixed and floating: within the ERM it is pegged against other EC currencies, and can only fluctuate within predetermined bands, while these currencies as a group float against others all over the world which are subject to **managed floating**.

Managed floating is sometimes known as 'dirty' floating, whereby governments intervene on foreign exchange markets to prevent sharp fluctuations by purchasing their own domestic currency when its value is falling and selling it when it is rising. This buying and selling can only take place if countries maintain sufficient reserves; if their reserves are insufficient they might have to borrow, and these borrowings might have strings attached. This happened in the late 1970s when the then Chancellor of the Exchequer in a Labour government was forced to impose a deflationary domestic policy involving cutbacks in government expenditure as a condition for receiving loans from the International Monetary Fund.

Arguments for and against floating exchange rates

In theory, floating exchange rates provide a means of eliminating balance of payments disequilibria. If the foreign exchange market were a completely free market (i.e. if governments made no attempt to influence exchange rates) the external value of a currency would change from day to day, and indeed from hour to hour and minute to minute in response to changes in supply and demand. These changes would, in theory, bring about *automatically* an adjustment to any disequilibrium in the balance of payments. If, for instance, the UK has a balance of payments deficit, then the value of sterling will depreciate in relation to other currencies. As discussed in Chapter 3, this will make UK exports cheaper and its imports dearer, thus tending to correct the disequilibrium. Again, as discussed in Chapter 3, the operation of this mechanism depends largely on elasticities: altering relative prices is one thing; how these price changes will translate into changes in the volume of exports and imports is another matter.

Governments have been reluctant to leave exchange rates completely to the mercy of the market for a number of reasons.

Firstly, the idea of an 'automatic' adjustment mechanism is attractive, but it ignores the fact that factors of production tend to be immobile. International exchange rate movements will favour some industries and penalize others, and if resources cannot be moved quickly between industries the government will be faced with a problem of structural unemployment.

Secondly, fluctuating exchange rates can reduce a government's ability to counteract unfavourable movements in the **terms of trade** (see Figure 11). When, for instance, competitiveness is reduced by a change in the terms of trade, a managed exchange rate can be adjusted to compensate.

Thirdly, floating exchange rates cause uncertainty. A UK travel operator, for example, when organizing package holidays in Spain, must

The **terms of trade index** is calculated as the ratio of export prices to import prices. A falling index means that more must be exported to purchase a given quantity of exports.

- Identify periods in Figure 11 when the UK terms of trade index deteriorated.
- What events in the world economy might explain these movements?

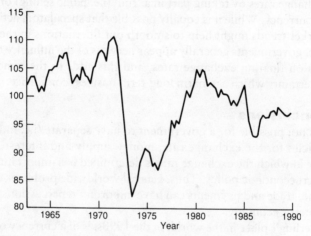

Figure 11 Terms of trade of the UK (1985 = 100)

negotiate the price of bedrooms with Spanish hoteliers well in advance of the summer season. He or she must also estimate transport costs in advance, and these costs are largely influenced by the price of aviation fuel, which is purchased internationally using dollars. Therefore changes in the exchange rate of sterling against the US dollar and the Spanish peseta can eliminate profit margins. Thus, during the period of 'dirty' floating in the 1970s, many holidaymakers found themselves being asked to pay quite substantial surcharges, allegedly due to unfavourable exchange rate movements (curiously, they never seemed to benefit from rebates due to favourable movements). Such uncertainty affected many sections of business, discouraging the placing of large orders and long-term trading agreements. However, there are ways of **hedging** some of the long-term risks – for instance, by insuring oneself against large exchange rate fluctuations, or by entering a 'forward' market where it is possible to agree in advance to purchase currency at a known price.

However, such arrangements come at a price and add to the transactions costs of international trade.

Fourthly, capital movements of a short-term nature, such as the transfer of 'hot money' from one country to another in a search for higher interest rates, can affect the exchange rate of a currency *even though the demand for and supply of goods and services has not changed*. Speculators can therefore be a special danger on freely floating foreign exchange markets where they might exaggerate fluctuations in exchange rates by taking part in a 'run' (i.e. panic selling) of a particular currency. While it is equally possible that speculators acting against market trends might help to smooth out fluctuations in the exchange rate, governments generally appear nervous of the influence of speculators on floating exchange rates, and this adds to the atmosphere of uncertainty which can harm long-term business confidence.

Conclusions

It is not possible for a government to have separate (i.e. independent) policies for the exchange rate, money supply and interest rates. The way in which the exchange rate is determined has important effects on macroeconomic policy. Thus, general worldwide problems of international trade and payments can have important repercussions on the UK domestic economy.

Sterling's place in the world, in the 1990s, is of a currency once of primary importance, now relegated to a secondary role. The world's major currencies, both for official reserves and for trading, are the deutschmark, dollar and yen. Sterling's exchange rates are major factors in UK competitiveness; and it has a new role as one of a number of 'weighted' currencies in the European Community's ECU 'basket', as discussed in the next chapter.

KEY WORDS

Gold standard	Bretton Woods
Reserve currencies	Fixed exchange rates
Sterling Area	Floating exchange rates
Exchange control	Managed floating
Hard currencies	Terms of trade (index)
Confidence	Hedging
Speculators	

Reading list
Curwen, P., ed., *Understanding the UK Economy*, Part 4, Macmillan, 1990.

Isaac, C., Chapter 23 in *Economics Now*, Stanley Thornes, 1986.

Morison, I. and Sheperdson, I., Chapters 2 and 6 in *Economics of the City*, Heinemann Educational, 1991.

Essay topics
1. (a) What are the main differences in the way the sterling exchange rate has been determined since 1972 when compared with the period from 1945 to 1972? (b) Consider the advantages and disadvantages of a return to the system prevailing before 1972. (Welsh Joint Education Committee, 1990)
2. How do the monetary authorities in the UK intervene in the foreign exchange market? Explain and comment on the reasons for such intervention. (University of Cambridge Local Examinations Syndicate, 1991)
3. 'British membership of the European Exchange Rate Mechanism is a strategy designed to reduce the rate of inflation at the expense of domestic output and employment.' Discuss. (Oxford & Cambridge Schools Examination Board, 1991)

Data Response Question 5

Government support for sterling
This task is based on a question set by the Welsh Joint Education Committee in 1991. The passage is an abstract of an article by Professor Milton Freidman, published in the *Financial Time*s on 18 December 1989. Study the passage and answer the following questions.

1. Why did the author assert that in effect a unified currency arrangement applied worldwide in the late nineteenth century?
2. What reasons might justify the author's assertion that a truly unified European currency would 'make a great deal of sense'?
3. Why does maintenance of pegged exchange rates between national currencies involve separate national central banks 'altering domestic monetary policy appropriately'?
4. What did the author mean when he argued that 'pressure to use monetary policy for domestic purposes will from time to time be irresistible'?
5. For what reasons could monetary policy used for domestic purposes cause the exchange system to become 'unstable'?

The case for floating rates

Discussions of the prospects for a monetary union within the Common Market have generally ignored the difference between two superficially similar but basically very different exchange rate arrangements.

One arrangement is a unified currency, the pound sterling in Scotland, England and Wales. Further back in time essentially the same arrangmeent applied in the late 19th century when pound, dollar, franc, etc., were simply different names for specified fixed amounts of gold. A truly unified European currency would make a great deal of sense.

An alternative arrangement is a system of exchange rates between national currencies pegged at agreed values to be maintained by the separate national central banks by altering domestic monetary policy appropriately.

Many proponents of a common European currency regard such a system of pegged exchange rates (the EMS) as a step towards a unified currency. I believe that is a grave mistake. In my opinion, a system of pegged exchange rates among national currencies is worse than either extreme, a truly unified currency, or national currencies linked by freely floating exchange rates. The reason is that national central banks will not, under modern conditions, be permitted to shape their policies with an eye solely to keeping the exchange rates of their currencies at the agreed level. Pressure to use monetary policy for domestic purposes will from time to time be irrestible. And when that occurs the exchange system becomes unstable.

That was certainly the experience under Bretton Woods. Even in its heyday, exchange rate changes were numerous and when they came often massive.

Experience since then has strengthened my confidence in a system of freely floating exchange rates, though it has also made me far more sceptical that such a system is politically feasible. Central banks will meddle, always of course with the best of intentions. None the less, even dirty floating exchange rates seem to me preferable to pegged rates, though not necessarily to a unified currency.

Chapter Six
The European dimension

'I don't care to belong to any organisation that would have me as a member.'   Groucho Marx

The European exchange rate mechanism
The European Monetary System (EMS) was established in March 1979 in order to encourage monetary stability and to discourage inflation in the EC. The Exchange rate mechanism (ERM) is part of the EMS, and represents a partial movement away from floating, as it is designed to keep European currencies exchanging with each other within agreed variations. Each country has a **central rate** against each of the others, set by the finance ministers and central banks of the participating countries. Most currencies are allowed to fluctuate within a narrow **band** of 2.25 per cent above or below their central rate, but at the time of writing both sterling and the peseta use a wider band of plus or minus 6 per cent. Currencies are kept within their bands by central bank intervention in the foreign exchange markets. If, for example, the pound falls to its lowest permitted level against the deutschmark, then the Bank of England, Bundesbank, and perhaps other central banks will buy pounds and sell deutschmarks to raise the value of sterling. Although central banks theoretically have access to unlimited short-term credit to finance such intervention, in practice a country will probably be reluctant to run up debts and will prefer to use interest rate adjustments to keep its currency within agreed bands. Eventually, therefore, it is hoped that all countries will find that the 'discipline' of the ERM will force all countries to take the necessary domestic measures to reduce their inflation rates – and hence interest rates – to the levels of the country with the lowest rates (currently Germany). It is possible for a government to agree to a realignment of its currency; and while many observers felt that sterling entered the ERM at an unrealistically high level, such realignments are, however, likely to be regarded as a sign of political and economic failure.

The UK in the ERM
On 8 October 1990, the then Chancellor of the Exchequer, John Major, announced that sterling would join the ERM. This move came

eleven years after the system began operating. The central rate against the deutschmark was £1 = DM2.95, with a 6 per cent band either side giving a range of DM2.78 to DM3.13. At the same time, the Chancellor was able to announce a 1 per cent cut in interest rates, thus bringing the possibility of lower mortgage rates for the first time in over two years. The announcement was made on the eve of a party conference, and was seen as a political move; but several economic arguments were also put forward for sterling's entry into the ERM.

It was suggested that there would be greater stability for sterling: that UK business would now be able to plan and invest for the future with greater certainty. It was also claimed that UK firms would find it more difficult to pass on higher wage costs to the customer in the form of higher prices. With a variable exchange rate, higher costs and higher export prices will tend to depress the currency and thus enable firms to continue selling exports because the fall in sterling would eliminate the output price disadvantage. This would not now happen with a fixed exchange rate, and thus the UK would ultimately achieve inflation rates in line with other European countries. A major disadvantage would be that the UK would suffer unemployment in those industries made internationally uncompetitive by what they might regard as an 'overvalued' sterling; and it was not long before a new Chancellor of the Exchequer was reported as stating that high levels of unemployment was a 'price worth paying' for European levels of inflation.

EMU and ECU

Monetary union has two main features. The first is that there is a **harmonization** of exchange rates, so that changes in the values of national currencies against each other are greatly reduced. Secondly, there is complete **convertibility** between currencies; i.e. any controls on exchanging currencies for either current or capital transactions are removed. If these two features were fully adopted within the EC it would mean, in effect, that producers would find that it would make little difference whether they sold their products in the UK, Ireland, Spain, or any other country; nor would they be particularly concerned whether they were paid in sterling, punts, pesetas or any other currency. It would make little difference, that is, from the point of view of using a medium of exchange. There would still, of course, be differences in transport costs, and costs in terms of the inconvenience of dealing in foreign languages, adapting to different scales of weights and measures, and so on. However, many of these inconveniences are scheduled to be removed during 1992. Thus the '**internal market**' measures due to come into full force by New Year's Day in 1993, removing barriers to the free movement of goods, services and factors of production between EC countries, would be supported by the free movement of currencies.

However, complete harmonization and convertibility still leaves substantial **transactions costs** in the form of commission charged by the banks and other agents who enable conversion to take place. Therefore the logic of monetary union appears to move inexorably towards the idea of a single European currency. Many observers feel that the debate which preoccupied the Conservative government in the UK in late 1991 regarding the stance of the UK towards a common currency was in many ways an artificial one, and that the sacrifice of 'national sovereignty' necessary to achieve monetary union is so significant that it is unrealistic for participating countries to resist the movement towards a single currency. This would eventually lead to a single central bank, a single monetary policy, and perhaps even a single finance minister for Europe: in other words, full political integration. Obviously, nationally based politicians might balk at this idea, but it is arguable that this is merely to deny the logical final outcome of policies which they are already pursuing.

The European Currency Unit (or **ECU**) is a currency 'basket' which is made up of national currencies in the proportions shown in the table in the boxed display.

THE ECU

The ECU is a composite or basket currency. It consists of specified *amounts* of each Community currency. The relative amounts of the component currencies roughly reflect their countries' economic weight and are normally revised every five years. The amounts were last changed in September 1989, when amongst other changes the ECU basket was enlarged to include the Spanish peseta and Portuguese escudo (see below). At present the deutschmark has a weight of around 30% in the ECU and sterling around 13%; however, even with unchanged amounts, the weights of the currencies constantly change as the currencies strengthen or weaken against each other.

The ECU's composition

Currency	Amount*	Weight(%)†
Belgian/Luxembourg franc	3.431	8.1
French franc	1.332	19.3
Lira	151.8	9.7
Guilder	0.2198	9.6
Deutschmark	0.6242	30.4
Danish krone	0.1976	2.5
Irish punt	0.008552	1.1
Peseta	6.885	5.2
Drachma	1.44	0.7
Pound sterling	0.08784	12.6
Escudo	1.393	0.8
		100.0

*these amounts have applied since September 1989.
†weights based on exchange rates on 30 October 1990.

Source: Bank of England *Fact Sheet*, November 1990

In order to find the value of the ECU in terms of, say, the pound sterling, it is necessary to convert each of the component parts into sterling at the current market exchange rate, and add them together. The ECU is therefore a simple 'weighted' average, the weights meant to be corresponding to the importance of each country in terms of the volume of trade within Europe.

As well as the 'official' ECU there is a market in a bond known as the 'unofficial' ECU, which is used by traders to settle international payments.

In 1989 the Delors Report argued that the ECU could develop into a currency in its own right, demonstrating the irreversibility of the move to monetary union, removing the transaction costs of converting currencies and making it considerably easier for the EC as a whole to manage its monetary policy. Within the EC the ECU is already the main unit of account in budgetary matters, and there is also a substantial number of businesses involved in international trade using the ECU as a medium of exchange. Opinion poll evidence suggests that tourists and travellers strongly support the idea of a single currency, and in its autumn 1991 conference, the Confederation of British Industry (CBI) confirmed that its policy was that the UK government should embrace a single European currency.

A European central bank

Discussion of a single currency for Europe leads naturally to discussion of a possible **European central bank**. A central bank is a feature of all developed countries, and is used by the government to control the system by which the supply of money is made available to the public and institutions. They have domestic responsibilities, such as controlling the credit creating activities of commercial banks, and international responsibilities in enabling international payments to be made. Their independence from the government varies from country to country; the German Bundesbank, which is specifically charged with the responsibility of conducting monetary policy so as to control inflation, is widely regarded as an institution with the degree of autonomy which would be appropriate for a European central bank.

Breaking down the barriers

The creation of a single market within the EC can be seen as a positive step towards free trade between nations, breaking down as it does artificial barriers and encouraging the free movement of labour and other factors of production. On the other hand, it can be seen as being part of a movement which might have damaging effects on wider world trade.

The European Economic Area

Before joining the EC, the UK was a member of the European Free Trade Association (EFTA). This organization was formed in 1959, and its other members were Norway, Sweden, Denmark, Austria, Portugal and Switzerland. Later, Leichtenstein, Finland and Iceland joined EFTA, but the UK, Denmark and Portugal left when they joined the EC.

EFTA is a **free trade area,** which means that its members agree to remove import tariffs on any goods originating in any other member country, but remain free to retain their own individual duties on goods imported from other countries. A free trade area needs to have rules preventing imports from non-member countries being sold in a high-tariff member country via a low-tariff member. Over the years these rules have been amended to enable EFTA countries and EC countries to trade more freely.

The EC, whose members are now the UK, France, Germany (including both west and east), Belgium, Netherlands, Luxembourg, Italy, Greece, Spain, Portugal, Denmark and Ireland, is a **customs union,** meaning that members eliminate tariffs for trade between them and, unlike a free trade area, maintain a common set of tariffs on trade with non-members.

In 1993, an integrated **European economic area,** linking the nineteen members of the EC and EFTA, is to be created so that the benefits of the single market measures of the EC can be extended to include all nineteen countries (see Figure 12). Whether the development of the EEA heralds a step towards the liberalization of world trade, or is a further symptom of the splintering of world trade into regional trading blocs, remains to be seen. The Uruguay Round of trade liberalization talks (see page 14) foundered over EC intransigence in refusing to make significant reductions to the CAP system of agricultural support, a system which flies in the face of Ricardian comparative advantage theory.

KEY WORDS	
EMS	Transactions costs
ERM	ECU
Central rate	European central bank
Band	EFTA
Harmonization	Free trade area
Convertibility	Customs union
Internal market	European economic area

Figure 12

Reading list

Bank of England, 'The European monetary system', *Fact Sheet*, November 1990.

Bank of England, 'European monetary arrangements', *Bank Briefing*, November 1991.

Healey, N. and Parker, D., Chapter 8 in *Current Topics in Economic Theory*, Anforme, 1990.

Hill, B., Chapter 6 in *The European Community*, Heinemann Educational, 1991.

Hitiris, T., 'A European central bank', *Economic Review*, January 1992.

Essay topics

1. Discuss the possible economic effects upon member countries resulting from the creation of a Single European Market within the European Community in 1992. (Associated Examining Board, 1990)

2. Examine the arguments for unrestricted international trade. In the light of these arguments, how would you justify the imposition of tariffs on US goods by the European Community? (University of London School Examinations Board, 1990)
3. In what ways do customs unions or free trade areas affect the gains from trade? (University of Oxford Delegacy of Local Examinations, 1989)
4. Compare the alternative ways open to a government to influence the level of economic activity. Explain what effect, if any, membership of the ERM has upon the government's choice of policy instruments. (Joint Matriculation Board, 1991)
5. Explain what is meant by the 'single European market'. Discuss how the standard of living in Europe in general, and that of Britain in particular, is likely to be affected by the single European market. (Joint Matriculation Board, 1991)

Data Response Question 6

Competition and innovation in the EC
This task is based on a question set by the Associated Examining Board in 1991. Study the article below, which is adapted from *Competition and Innovation* by G.A. Geroski, a discussion document prepared for the Commission of the European Communities. Answer the following questions.

1. Explain in your own words, what the writer means by the terms: (i) dynamic efficiency; (ii) static efficiency; and (iii) monopoly power.
2. Explain why it seems reasonable to argue that: (i) 'increases in market size will increase innovation'; and (ii) 'large firms with at least some degree of monopoly power are likely to be most innovative'.
3. Discuss the view that removing all barriers to trade within the EC will bring substantial gains to all member states.

There are a number of obstacles which restrict trade within the European Community, and there are good reasons to think that removing them may bring substantial gains to all member states. Policies have been suggested to tackle these problems, and if adopted they are likely to improve the allocation of resources within the European Community.

The primary effects of reducing the barriers to trade between countries who are members of the European Community will be an increase in market size and in the amount of competition in the enlarged market. These changes are likely to affect the efficiency of firms and the performance of markets in several different ways. When examining these effects, it is necessary to distinguish between dynamic efficiency and static efficiency.

Improvements in dynamic efficiency will result if the removal of barriers to trade leads to invention, innovation and a faster rate of technological change. However, even if these long run benefits do not occur it is still almost certain that there will be improvements in static efficiency. A larger market and more competition is likely to result in a better allocation of resources, even if the pace of technological change is unaffected. The only controversy is about the size of the benefits which will result from these improvements in static efficiency.

A larger market and the resulting increase in demand will allow firms with unexploited economies of scale to move down their long run average cost curves. More competition is also likely to encourage firms to reduce inefficiency and to produce whatever output they choose, at the lowest average cost. These two effects lead to the prediction that costs are likely to fall as the size of the market and the degree of competition increase.

The effects of market size and competition on dynamic efficiency, however, are much less clear. Certainly it seems reasonable to suggest that increases in market size will increase innovation, particularly if there are any economies of scale or fixed costs in the research and development process. However the effect of competition on innovation is rather controversial, some economists believe that large firms with at least some degree of monopoly power are likely to be most innovative. If this is true, it is not certain that removing the barriers to trade between the members of the European Community will improve dynamic efficiency. Indeed it is possible that the static efficiency gains will be more than outweighed by the losses arising from a reduction in dynamic efficiency.

Chapter Seven

Trade as a problem

'*Some may be puzzled why the existence of a current account deficit is so newsworthy in the United Kingdom. The truth is we are prisoners of the past...*' Nigel Lawson

Are current account deficits a problem?

In Chapter 1, we saw that the distinction between domestic trade and international trade is largely unreal, because most trade takes place between individuals. It is possible to take this view a stage further and to argue that current account deficits do not matter, since they arise out of private transactions and, being the result of the purchasing decisions of millions of individuals, they merely reflect market conditions.

Attention has been drawn to the fact that balance of payments statistics are not always reliable. Within the UK figures, the size of the 'balancing item' suggests major inaccuracies. Also, consider Table 7 – the overall balance of payments of the world does not always balance! Since we have not yet developed trade links with Mars or Venus this must cast some doubts on the seriousness with which we should take the figures. It has happened in the UK on more than one occasion that a Chancellor of the Exchequer has taken quite significant decisions on the basis of balance of payments deficits which, in later years, were revised by the statisticians, when further information came to light – and turned out to be surpluses!

Table 7 World current balances ($ billion)

United States	−110	−99	−9
Japan	57	36	41
OECD Europe	7	−1	−34
of which: Germany	57	48	0
Total OECD	−78	−94	−26
OPEC	−2	14	−31
Latin America	−9	−13	−13
Four Asian NIEs	24	15	11
Other non-OECD countries	−19	−4	−26
World total	−85	−82	−84

Source: OECD *Economic Outlook,* July 1991

One way of establishing whether the balance of payments really matters is to examine the **absorption approach**. The absorption approach to the analysis of balance of payments deficits is based on the national income identity:

$$Y = C + I + G + X - M,$$

where Y is national income, C is consumption expenditure, I is investment, G is government spending on goods and services, X is exports and M is imports. The equation can be rewritten as:

$$Y - D = X - M,$$

where D is domestic expenditure (or 'absorption'). Now the equation suggests that a deficit on the balance of payments will exist where the country 'absorbs' more goods and services than it produces; i.e. when D is greater than Y.

Since $C = Y - S - T$, where S is saving and T is taxation, the absorption formula can be rewritten as:

$$(I - S) + (G - T) = (M - X).$$

This equation suggests that a current account deficit can be linked to an increase in investment or a fall in saving, and that it can also be associated with a budget deficit; i.e. the government spending more than it receives in revenue. This budget deficit is usually financed through government borrowing, which according to critics of such 'deficit financing' is not only inflationary, but has the side-effect of 'crowding out' private sector borrowing for investment purposes. The USA experienced some hefty **'twin deficits'** during the 1980s, and were it not for revenues from North Sea oil and the selling of privatization shares, the UK would undoubtedly have had worse problems of this type.

In a sense, then, a current account deficit is a sign of **'dis-saving'** by either the private or public sector. Private dis-saving arises either because companies believe that the rate of return from investment in the future will exceed the cost of borrowing and investing now, or because individuals decide that they prefer present to future consumption. Conservative Chancellors of the Exchequer suggested in the late 1980s that the so-called current account deficit 'problem' is in fact a debt-related problem: it arises from the fact that deficits add to a country's overseas debt and impose a burden on future generations for the consumption of the present generation. They further argued that whether this truly constitutes a 'problem' depends largely upon what the deficit is used for. If it is used for consumption, then the burden can feed upon itself and increase as time goes on. But if it is used for production (e.g. the importation of machine parts or raw materials for processing) then the debt can be repaid out of future exports and the debt can be serviced using future output. Supporters of the Conservative government view would argue that providing the government's own finances are in balance, then there should be nothing to worry about in the balance of payments figures, and deficits are likely to be temporary. Professor Patrick Minford, for instance, even suggested at one stage that the record balance of payments deficits were a sign of success as they indicated that raw materials were being imported as a basis for subsequent exports.

Critics of the government pointed out that the resulting export boom seemed to be a long time in coming and that by 1991 the balance of payments deficits appeared to be anything but 'temporary'. They also pointed out that the budget surpluses of the 1980s were largely financed by once-and-for-all revenues from the privatization of nationalized industries, and accused the government of short-termism in allowing a consumer credit boom which sucked in imports. They rejected the notion that a private sector deficit was 'good' while a public sector deficit was 'bad'. Rather, it depended on what the deficit was used for: riotous living, causing a burden on future generations, or seedcorn investment with an eye to the future.

If the balance of payments position does not matter, then it could be argued that exchange rates similarly do not matter. Since an exchange rate is arguably a mere technical item which reflects a country's trading position, it could be regarded as simply being the price of the domestic currency on exchange markets, and its maintenance at a predetermined level need not be exalted to the status of a sacred cow as an overriding aim of policy. Curiously, the persons who argue that balance of payments deficits are unimportant tend to be the very same who attach a great deal of importance to the exchange rate, and they often appear to regard a devaluation as at worst a national disgrace, at best a loss of virility. Notice the value judgements which slip into economic journalism in such a Freudian way every day when describing a rising currency as 'strong' and a falling currency as 'weak'. Politicians are adept, of course, at holding two or three conflicting opinions simultaneously, and so perhaps we should not be surprised that such people can with one breath argue that international trading transactions are 'merely' reflections of private sector decisions, and with the next breath suggest that the position of sterling in the world is not only vital to the UK economy but is central to issues of national sovereignty.

In *Deindustrialization* by Stephen Bazen and Tony Thirlwall (a companion volume in this series), it is argued that a current account deficit

Is there a balance of payments crisis?

PATRICK MINFORD

We have had some bad trade figures recently. Could these be a problem? There was a time when bad trade figures quickly led to crisis and policy change. This was under the Bretton Woods system of the adjustable exchange rate peg (sometimes called 'fixed' exchange rates), which prevailed up to 1970 from the Second World War. Then the rules were that a country must keep its current account in steady balance. If it could not, it must devalue or deflate the economy in the event of a deficit, and vice versa for a surplus. So bad trade figures started immediate speculation about devaluation and this in turn caused a decrease in the demand for pounds, causing a run on the reserves and possibly precipitating the devaluation and other policy changes.

Nowadays, the rules are different; there are no agreed rules of international behaviour at all. Whether a trade deficit will cause policy change and if so just what, is a matter for decision by the government concerned. This is illustrated by this government's reaction to the recent figures. It clearly plans no policy change; the market, accordingly, is not concerned. There is no crisis.

Another difference between today and twenty years ago is the state of our net foreign assets. They now stand at £114 billion; then they stood at a mere £1.5 billion. World markets then wanted quick action to stop a possible move into debt. Now, as the second largest creditor nation, we can call the tune.

But the government could eventually be forced to take action if poor figures persist. The reason is that a persistent current deficit would steadily erode our net foreign assets, and this cannot continue indefinitely. Either British consumers will be getting poorer which must reduce their spending and with it their imports (that would automatically correct the deficit) or, if the source of the deficit lies in government's own budget deficits, the rising foreign debt will be mirrored in rising government debt; and then it will be the government that is forced to act to correct its own deficit, *by cutting spending or raising taxes*. Monetary policy will not do so. In the case of a current account deficit (arising from either consumer or government deficits), a tightening of monetary policy (higher interest rates) does not address the source of the current account crisis, and simply increases the willingness of private investors to buy sterling assets, thereby reducing the need to finance the current account deficit from the central bank reserves.

There is both good theory and evidence that the private sector does not run persistent deficits; basically any such tendency would be self-correcting as their spending will reflect their wealth, including foreign assets. So the source of persistent deficits will be the government's own deficit. Even this, as we have seen, must be corrected; but the political process could delay adjustment, and precipitate eventual crisis. So one way to judge whether we have such a potential crisis is to look at the government's own finances. Are these out of balance?

It does not seem so. The PSBR is expected to be less than 1% of GDP during 1987, possibly only 0.5% or even in surplus, according to some estimates. Revenues are strong and the following year the PSBR would almost certainly be in surplus without tax cuts. Even excluding privatisation revenues, since these are temporary, the PSBR is only slightly higher and moving strongly towards surplus.

If the private sector keeps itself in balance over the medium term and government is keeping its finances in balance, then there should be nothing to worry about in the trade figures. If they are in deficit, it is likely to be temporary.

This is just what it seems to be. Britain is currently growing faster than elsewhere, but that will not persist as other countries recover. Our exports will then pick up.

What is more, there is a lot of doubt about whether we are in deficit at all. The invisibles are thought by some City analysts to be understated. And some argue that exports are also under-recorded at present. These two things could account partly for the large balancing item in our total payments accounts; this measure of missing current and capital account items is now no less than £12 billion. All in all, it is only sensible to keep calm about these trade figures. Crisis? What crisis? Fair enough, on this occasion.

Source: *Economic Review*, January 1988

Why the balance of payments matters

TONY THIRLWALL

It became fashionable in the 1980s, when Nigel Lawson was Chancellor, to say that the balance of payments does not matter as long as it is not associated with a budget deficit and is voluntarily financed so that a payments deficit is purely a private matter of no public concern.

There is a fundamental fault with this argument. Private agents do not determine the rate of interest, the Government and the Bank of England determine interest rates – and the balance of payments position and associated pressure on the exchange rate are crucial in determining what the nominal and real rate of interest will be.

Interest rates, in turn, affect the functioning of the real economy by influencing the willingness to invest. The state of the balance of payments, therefore, has economic and social repercussions extending far beyond the free choice exercised by economic agents about how much they wish to spend and to borrow from abroad.

Rates were gradually reduced in the early 1980s as the balance of payments improved and inflation was brought under control through the crude weapon of unemployment. But they were raised again from the mid-1980s as the balance of payments plunged into deficit. Since 1982 the virtually continuous rise in real interest rates has been the mirror image of the deterioration of the balance of payments position in relation to GDP.

It is difficult to know precisely what damage interest rate oscillations have done to the economy but if Britain had not experienced balance of payments difficulties as soon as growth approached the rates of its competitors and go-stop avoided, the macro-economy would surely be healthier.

It is not coincidental, for example, that in the 1980s the highest real interest rates in post-war history coincided with zero net investment in manufacturing industry. It was more profitable to hold monetary assets than to invest in plant and machinery.

In the history of economic thought, part of the mercantilist argument was that a strong balance of payments would keep interest rates low and benefit the real economy. This was a central element of Keynes's defence of mercantilism in the 1930s.

Today, 'mercantilist' is used as a term of abuse. Like the mercantilists of old, those who stress the importance of the balance of payments for the real economy are accused of being anti-free trade and confusing money and real wealth.

This is unfair. What both the old and latter-day mercantilists recognise is that the short-term rate of interest is a monetary phenomenon and that it can be too high in relation to the needs of growth and full employment.

The rate of interest required for external equilibrium – to finance deficits and/or to stop the currency collapsing – may be way above that required for internal equilibrium, as we have witnessed in the UK, especially during the past three years.

Nominal interest rates have recently come down as a result of the prolonged recession that has dampened inflation and improved the balance of payments by restricting imports. But we are oceans away from simultaneous internal and external equilibrium.

With the Government's commitment to the exchange rate mechanism of the European Monetary System, Britain is now locked into a system not dissimilar to the gold exchange standard of the Bretton Woods era of 1944–1971 – which, ironically, many of the current supporters of the ERM did their best to undermine in the 1960s – or to the pre-1931 gold standard of fixed exchange rates.

What is currently happening in the UK is reminiscent of what Keynes felt about economic policy in the 1920s when, in his polemic against the return to the gold standard at the pre-war parity in 1925, he described monetary policy as 'simply a campaign against the standard of living of the working classes' operating through the 'deliberate intensification of unemployment . ... a policy which the country would never permit if it knew what was being done.'

It is not the magic wand of the ERM that has brought inflation down to 4 per cent, but the chronic unemployment caused by high interest rates that has knocked the stuffing out of the trade union movement. When recovery comes, there is nothing to stop inflation accelerating again and the balance of payments deteriorating. Interest rates will be raised again and the vicious circle of high interest rates, weak investment, recession and rising unemployment will start once more.

Until policies are designed to improve the balance of payments to allow a sustainable growth rate of at least 2.5 per cent, ERM membership will imply continued high interest rates and high unemployment throughout the 1990s. Those who argue that the current account of the balance of payments does not matter must answer the mercantilist charge.

Source: *Observer*, 29 December 1991

on the balance of payments *does* matter: firstly because it results in interest rates being higher than they otherwise would be, with harmful effects on investment, and the long-term modernity of the capital stock of the country. Secondly, it matters because the UK is missing out on the possibility of economic growth led by exports. According to this argument, 'lumping the capital and current account of the balance of payments together, and saying there is no problem because the balance of payments must always balance, is to bury one's head in the sand as far as the functioning of the real economy is concerned.' Compare the two extracts on pages 63 and 64 (from Professors Minford and Thirlwall) which give opposite views of whether the balance of payments matters.

As was argued in Chapter 3, the balance of payments figures do not just represent an accounting exercise. Problems arise from the *strain of the balancing act*, and these problems result at the very least in a loss of jobs. The effect of job losses, furthermore, is often more severe in those regions of the country which are already economically disadvantaged. In terms of economic problems and opportunities, balance of payments deficits aggravate what the National Institute of Economic and Social research has called the 'regional mismatch' of the UK.

UK invisible earnings

We saw in Chapter 3 that, in many years, the balance of invisibles has been sufficient to compensate for a deficit on visible trade. Between 1986 and 1987, however, the scale of the recession was such that invisibles no longer performed this function. The recession which gripped the UK throughout 1990–92 affected not only the factories of Wigan or Merthyr Tydfil, but also the financial offices of Reading and even the supermarkets of Guildford.

International trade has important effects on domestic employment. Economists have often suggested that 'export-led growth' is a means of expanding the economy without causing inflation. The fact that the UK has traditionally had a positive balance of invisibles has given some economists and politicians the idea that a decline in employment in manufacturing can be more than compensated for by an expansion of the service sector. Others are somewhat disturbed by the idea that a country can rely on a service sector to rescue it from economic decline, and that manufacturing can somehow be written off. The service sector does not exist in isolation. It must be remembered that many services are what are often known as 'aids to trade'. If manufacturing declines, then so does the demand for transport, insurance and banking; and eventually so does the demand of businesses for corporate entertainment and hospitality through hotels and catering. An economy which does not have a 'value-added' sector, taking raw materials and turning them into final products, cannot sustain a tertiary sector in the long run.

According to Bazen and Thirlwall, in *Deindustrialization*, there are two definitions of deindustrialization: a declining *share* of total employment in manufacturing; and an *absolute* decline in employment in manufacturing. The first is an experience common to most developed economies; the second, however, can be a cause for concern. Countries like Japan have used productivity increases to support higher levels of total output from existing workers. This can be represented by AB in Figure 13 and is known as **positive deindustrialization**. It is very rare for Japanese firms to lay off workers. In the UK in the 1980s, however, productivity has increased, while fewer people have been employed and total output has been stagnant and even fallen. This is represented by AC in the figure, and is known as **negative deindustrialization**.

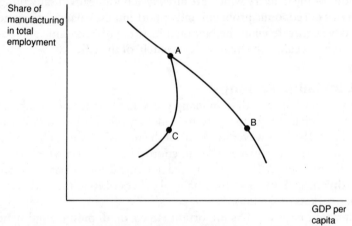

Figure 13 Positive and negative deindustrialization

Negative deindustrialization occurs where there is a decline in the share of manufacturing in total employment, and where the labour displaced results in unemployment rather than being absorbed into the non-manufacturing sectors. Deindustrialization can therefore be associated with benefits if it is accompanied by fast output growth, or cause severe problems if it is associated with stagnant growth. Bazen and Thirlwall argue that UK deindustrialization has been of the negative kind. I would add to this that UK deindustrialization has not been caused by any overall lack of demand. The balance of payments figures show that demand for goods in the UK is strong, at least as strong as the demand for services. In the mid-1980s, however, the deregulation of the financial markets and the availability of easy credit led to a consumer boom. This boom did not benefit UK manufacturers to any great degree. It was essentially the retail sector which benefited in the short run. In the West Midlands, the Round Oak Steelworks became the Merryhill Shopping Centre; in South Wales the Swansea Enterprise Zone, which was supposed to benefit manufacturers with an area free from planning regulations, filled up with retail warehouses relocated from the city centre. And when customers filed through the checkouts to pay for their TV sets, clothes, computers or pine furniture with their credit cards, their purchases were more likely to be adding to the gross domestic product of Japan or Taiwan than the UK. The argument boils down to this: services *are* important because the demand for services is high; but (apart from when the government deliberately creates a recession) the demand for goods is also high. Whereas the UK has always been regarded as an efficient provider of services, there is now a failure to supply goods.

On the other hand, a provocative and subversive view has been put forward by the *Economist* newspaper:

> '*Manufacturing is not uniquely important, nor is all manufacturing important, nor is manufacturing necessarily the most important activity*'.

Do you agree? Look again at Chapter 3, at UK trends in visibles and invisibles.

KEY WORDS

Absorption approach	Positive deindustrialization
Twin deficits	Negative deindustrialization
Dis-saving	

Reading list

Bazen, S. and Thirlwall, T., Chapter 2 in *Deindustrialization*, 2nd edn, Heinemann Educational, 1992.

Healey, N.M., 'Do current account deficits matter?', *Economic Review*, March 1991.

Healey, N.M., 'Does the UK current account matter?', *British Economy Survey*, spring 1990.

Wells, J., 'The economy after 10 years: stronger or weaker?', *Journal of the Economics Association*, winter 1989.

Essay topics

1. Discuss whether a balance of payments deficit poses problems for the UK economy. Critically compare different ways in which a payments deficit may be reduced. (Associated Examining Board, 1990)
2. During the 1980s, the UK's balance of trade in manufactured goods has moved from surplus into deficit. Explain why, and discuss whether it matters. (Associated Examining Board, 1989)
3. Explain what you understand by 'deindustrialization'. What are the potential benefits of deindustrialization to an economy? (Southern Universities Joint Board, 1989)
4. What do you consider to be the main consequences for an economy of a sustained deterioration in its terms of trade? (Oxford & Cambridge Schools Examination Board, 1989)

Data Response Question 7

Deindustrialization
This task is based on a question set by the Oxford & Cambridge Schools Examination Board in 1990. Study Table A, which is derived from data in CSO *National Income and Expenditure: Employment Gazette* and *British Business*, and then answer the questions.

Table A Deindustrialization in the United Kingdom

	1979	1986	1988
Index of manufacturing output (1980 = 100)	109.5	104.7	118.7
Share of manufacturing in total output (%)	27.3	23.0	23.9
Employment in manufacturing (thousands)	7259	5239	5152
Share of manufacturing in total employment (%)	31.3	24.3	22.7
Employment in services (thousands)	13 556	14 495	15 319
Share of services in total employment (%)	58.5	67.1	69.5
Balance of trade in manufactures (£ million)	+2698	−8055	−15 770
UK import penetration in manufactures (%)	26	33	38

1. Define 'deindustrialization'.
2. What symptoms of deindustrialization appear in the data in Table A? Is there any evidence of its causes?
3. Are the trends a cause for concern?

Chapter Eight

UK trade and demand side policy

'In the wake of the Keynesian revolution, the state undertakes to regulate the total income available for the purchase of goods and services . . .' John Kenneth Galbraith

Policy on the demand side

Demand management policies aim to influence the level of economic activity by increasing or reducing the level of **aggregate demand**.

Aggregate demand consists of consumption, investment, government expenditure, and exports net of imports. The **multiplier** principle tells us that any increase (or decrease) in aggregate demand can be expected to increase (or decrease) national income by an amount greater than the initial change in aggregate demand.

Macroeconomic objectives

Oversight of the UK's trading position, its balance of payments and the sterling exchange rate is only one area of macroeconomic concern for policy makers. Chancellors of the Exchequer and other government finance ministers are a little like performers we used to see at the circus: spinning plates on top of wobbly poles. Their plates are labelled 'low inflation', 'full employment', 'steady growth' and 'balance of payments equilibrium'. The trick is to keep them all spinning, and the problem is that if you devote too much attention to one, another comes crashing down.

For the 25 years preceding the Second World War, the unemployment rate in the UK averaged 13 per cent, and at its peak was 22 per cent. During the first 25 years following the war (before the 'stagflation' of the 1970s), unemployment averaged 1.5 per cent. This remarkable contrast was brought about by the use of Keynesian demand management techniques.

The relationship of demand management policies to particular problem areas is summarized in the 'Keynesian grid' shown in Table 8. The first column shows five different 'problem areas'. The inclusion of a balance of payments surplus as a 'problem' would cause some surprise among those of a 'mercantilist' persuasion (see page 64), but in Chapter

3 it was argued that surpluses are not necessarily desirable in a world of interdependent trading partners.

Table 8 The 'Keynesian grid'

Problem area	Monetary policy	Budgetary policy	Direct policy
Inflation	Restrictive	Deflationary	Prices and incomes
Balance of payments deficit (falling £)	Restrictive	Deflationary	Prices and incomes, import controls, devaluation
Balance of payments surplus (rising £)	Expansive	Reflationary	Revaluation
Unemployment	Expansive	Reflationary	Incomes policy without price controls
Low growth	Expansive	Reflationary	Remove controls

A balance of payments deficit, which has had more than academic interest for the UK in recent years, can be tackled on the demand management side of the economy by using two broad sets of policies. One is known as **expenditure reduction** – i.e. deflationary policies reducing the demand for all products, including imports; or **expenditure switching**, where the pattern of consumption is influenced so that home-produced goods are substituted for imports. Devaluation of the currency is an expenditure-switching policy, and others might include import controls or export incentives encouraging producers to sell their output overseas rather than on the domestic market.

Conflict between policy objectives

Table 8 also shows how it is possible to be faced with problems requiring opposite solutions – for example, where a balance of payments deficit occurs at the same time as unemployment and low growth. Here, the 'direct policies' column provides some flexibility, and a devaluation of the currency would be recommended by neo-Keynesian policy advisers as a means of stimulating export-led growth. This assumes, of course, that the government has direct control over the exchange rate; but membership of exchange rate mechanisms such as that of the European Monetary System reduces this flexibility and steers the government towards a narrower range of options, such as reliance on the 'single golf club' of the interest rate. Prices and incomes policies might provide some potential for further flexibility, but support for their introduction seems to wax and wane, as they go in and out of fashion.

Why do policies conflict?

Stable prices will enable a country to compete in export markets and achieve equilibrium in the balance of payments. A country in a strong trading position can develop without restricting real incomes, and thus a buoyant level of demand can maintain full employment. Why, then, do the aims of macroeconomic policy sometimes appear to be incompatible? Why cannot all macroeconomic aims be achieved by a single all-embracing policy? The answer is that measures to achieve one objective often prevent the achievement of another in the short run. As indicated by the neo-Keynesian box, for instance, tax reductions aimed at increasing employment through higher aggregate demand might have the effect of increasing expenditure on imports, and thus causing balance of payments problems; increased interest rates aimed at reducing aggregate demand and discouraging imports might have the effect of increasing the exchange rate and so make it more difficult to sell exports.

Neo-Keynesian analysis stresses the idea of '**trade-offs**'. Keynes himself realized that running a budget deficit in order to reduce unemployment could be inflationary, but he regarded a mild rate of inflation as an acceptable price to pay for achieving full employment. You will undoubtedly examine this trade-off during your studies using the **Phillips curve**, which is fully discussed in *UK Unemployment* by Andrew Clark and Richard Layard, a companion volume in this series. Figure 14 shows the trade-off between full employment and equilibrium in the balance of payments, which has been another significant part of the economic history of the UK, a trading nation with a relatively high propensity to import.

Let us assume that the economy depicted in Figure 14 is operating below its full-employment level of income (that is to say, there is always spare capacity to enable more goods and services to be produced). National income is in equilibrium where aggregate demand equals aggregate supply at Y_{E1}. We assume here that exports are exogenously determined (they do not depend on the national income of the country in question; rather they are determined by incomes in other countries). It is reasonable to suppose that imports are endogenously determined (they increase with national income) since higher incomes will enable people to afford to purchase increased quantities of goods and services

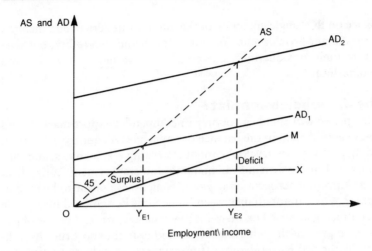

Figure 14 Conflict between increased employment and
balance of payments (internal and external balance)

from abroad. For the sake of simplicity, we assume that the imports
graph is a straight line rising from the origin.

At Y_{E1} there is a *balance of payments surplus*, because exports are
greater than imports at this level of income. Suppose aggregate demand
is now increased, perhaps through a cut in direct taxes which increases
disposable income and hence increases consumption, or through an
increase in government spending or investment which increases income
and expenditure through a multiplier effect. The line AD_1 shifts to
AD_2. However, some of the increased demand will be reflected in
higher spending on imports.

At the new equilibrium level of income Y_{E2} there is a *balance of payments deficit*. This move from surplus into deficit will be more pro-
nounced if the country has a high **marginal propensity to import** and
the gradient of the M function is therefore greater. This diagram is
illustrative of the tendency of the UK economy to experience '**stop-go**'
cycles, as increased incomes tend to 'suck in' imports, leading the government of the day to introduce measures to reduce the level of aggregate demand in the short run, but sacrificing output and economic
growth in the long run.

Demand management and 'stop–go' policies
If trade-offs are necessary, then economic policy ceases to be a purely
technical matter and it enters the political arena. It does this because it
becomes necessary to choose between priorities, and this is the job of

the politician rather than the economist. British experience since the Second World War illustrates some of the difficulties in making choices between priorities.

From 1945 to about 1964 inflation rates were very low, and priority was given to achieving full employment. During the 1950s the policy of 'stop–go' came to characterize Britain's efforts to achieve economic growth. More correctly, the phrase should be 'go–stop', because the typical sequence of events was that a consumer boom would be allowed to build up, to be followed by drastic deflationary policies to curb an influx of imports and a run on sterling.

From 1964 to 1969 the achievement of a balance of payments surplus was a main objective of the policy of Harold Wilson's Labour government, and this was tackled to a large extent by sacrificing growth. Between 1969 and 1971, owing to restricted aggregate demand and devaluation, Britain had the largest balance of payments surplus and the highest unemployment since 1938.

Between 1971 and 1974, the Conservative government of Edward Heath concentrated on foreign policy almost to the exclusion of everything else and arguably subjugated all other considerations to the overriding aim of entering the EC. In order to attempt to match the level of economic activity then being experienced by EC countries, the government made its famous 'bolt for growth', followed by its equally famous 'U turn' when international factors (particularly the OPEC oil price rise) created both inflation and deflation simultaneously.

An explanation is needed of the suggestion that the five-fold increase in the world price of oil between 1974 and 1975 was both inflationary and deflationary. It was *inflationary* because it raised the costs of industry, and so contributed to cost-push inflation. It was *deflationary* because of its effect on aggregate demand and unemployment. The neo-Keynesian box, which assumes that problems will occur in groups of two, or three at the most, clearly cannot cope very comfortably with 'stagflation' of this sort. Britain suffered record inflation at the same time as high unemployment, balance of payments deficits and low growth, and it seemed to many as if the traditional Keynesian idea of 'trade-offs' had broken down. This led some economists, notably the monetarists, to attempt to completely discredit Keynesian policy and to seek radical alternatives. Harold Wilson's second period in office as Labour Prime Minister saw the introduction of tighter monetary controls, but it was only after the election of Margaret Thatcher's Conservative government in 1979 that fully-fledged monetarist policies were experimented with on a large scale. Priority was thus given to tackling inflation, and it was argued that the achievement of other macroeconomic policies would only be possible once price stability was achieved. For a time, North Sea oil exports tended to disguise a decline in Britain's exporting industries; but many have argued that this decline was actually accelerated by the high sterling price caused by oil surpluses.

'Monetarism' – in the narrowest sense of attempting to control inflation through achieving monetary targets – was abandoned after only a few years, mainly because it was incompatible with the intention of the Thatcher government to 'liberalize' the money and capital markets. However, in broader terms 'monetarism' survived, and was rechristened by some as 'Thatcherism', encompassing accelerating privatization and a heavy reliance on market forces in all aspects of life.

In the early 1990s, it has become possible once again to identify 'trade-offs', now that expectations have settled at higher levels than existed two decades ago – when interest rates in double figures, for instance, would have been unthinkable. At the time of writing it is possible to detect an increased concern for priorities other than stable prices, and there is also an increased interest from all sections of the political spectrum in the development of long-term supply side policies.

KEY WORDS

Demand management	Expenditure switching
Aggregate demand	Trade-offs
Multiplier	Phillips curve
Macroeconomic objectives	Marginal propensity to import
Expenditure reduction	Stop–go

Reading list

Clark, A. and Layard, R., Chapter 2 in *UK Unemployment*, 2nd edn, Heinemann Educational, 1992.

Harrison, B., Smith, C. and Davies, B., Chapter 36 in *Introductory Economics*, Macmillan, 1992.

Smith, D., *Mrs Thatcher's Economics: Her Legacy*, Heinemann Educational, 1992.

Essay topics

1. (a) Distinguish between monetary policy and fiscal policy. (b) How might monetary and fiscal policy be used to reduce a balance of payments deficit? (Associated Examining Board, 1991)

2. Compare different policies that a government might pursue to eliminate a large and persistent deficit on the current account of the balance of payments. (Associated Examining Board, 1991)
3. What do you understand by the phrase 'conflict of policy objectives?' To what extent is the UK's ability to pursue domestic economic policies limited by balance of payments constraints? (University of London School Examinations Board, 1991)

Data Response Question 8

Pressure on sterling
This task is based on a question set by the University of London School Examinations Board in 1991. Read the passage, which is adapted from an article in *The Times* of 7 October 1989, and answer the following questions.

1. Explain how a boom may lead to 'accelerating pay settlements, a huge balance of payments deficit, pressure on sterling and a rising rate of inflation'.
2. Examine the meaning and significance of the following statement: 'The trick here includes keeping the pound from falling and continuing to attract enough short term foreign money to cover the balance of payments deficit'.
3. The above extract was written a year before the government announced that the UK would join the exchange rate mechanism (ERM). How does membership of the ERM affect the determination of monetary policy in the UK?

Interest rates reached a low of $7\frac{1}{2}$ per cent following the 1988 Budget, the same Budget that lured thousands of first-time buyers into the housing market.

The legacy of the 1987–88 boom is a familiar one: accelerating pay settlements, a huge balance of payments deficit, pressure on sterling and a rising rate of inflation. Unfortunately only time will tell if the only cure can be recession. Interest rates are now higher than at any time since November 1981 when Sir Geoffrey Howe deliberately drove the economy deeper into recession and gave Mrs Thatcher her initial victory over inflation. The chosen instrument now, as then, is high interest rates.

So far the measures used have not restrained demand sufficiently. Consumer spending has continued to rise. Unemployment is still falling and pay settlements are rising. Will interest rates at 15 per cent do the trick? The trick here includes keeping the pound from falling and continuing to attract enough short term foreign money to cover the balance of payments deficit.

Chapter Nine
UK trade and supply side policy

'Supply creates its own demand.'   Jean-Baptiste Say

Supply side policy
The decline of UK plc is not new. In 1851 Prince Albert, the husband of Queen Victoria, promoted the Great Exhibition at the Crystal Palace which then stood in London's Hyde Park. It was meant to show off British wares to the world, but it also had the effect of warning British industrialists how rapidly their technologies were falling behind those of other countries, particularly at that time Germany. Prime Minister William Gladstone later initiated an enquiry into the education system in Britain to try to discover whether changes could improve Britain's economic performance. Since then, Britain's relative economic decline has been an issue at virtually every general election, especially in the second half of the twentieth century.

In 1850, the UK had 41 per cent of world trade in manufactures; this fell to 14 per cent by 1960, 9 per cent in 1970 and 6 per cent in 1991. In 1945, the UK had the third highest GDP per head among industrialized nations; in 1991 the country had slipped to fourteenth place (see Figure 15). For over 100 years governments of different political complexions have come and gone, but UK growth rates have persistently hovered at averages of 2–3 per cent a year, while European rates have usually been at higher levels. These statistics trace a path of decline through the economic league tables.

UK economic growth
Economic growth occurs when a country increases its productive capacity and its national income. The rate of increase of the national income of a country provides some indication of the standard of living of its people.

The determinants of economic growth include the quantity and quality of a country's factors of production: whether its labour force is well skilled; whether its capital equipment is efficient, and so on. It also depends on the availability of natural resources, the state of technical knowledge, such matters as the country's political stability, and the

76

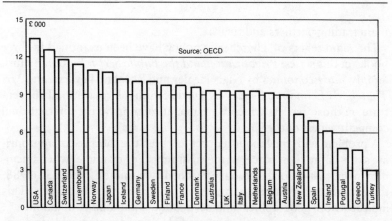

Figure 15 GDP per head in OECD countries in 1990

attitude of the public to such influences as investment and entrepreneurship. In making international comparisons, however, it is necessary to examine national income *levels*, as well as rates of growth. The fact that developing countries like Korea can achieve far higher rates of growth than the UK is significant for the countries concerned, as it means that on the whole their citizens can hope to achieve higher living standards; but it has less significance for already developed countries like the UK. A relatively small percentage growth rate in the UK represents a far higher *absolute* increase in national income compared with most developing countries which are starting from a much lower base.

So where is the UK? On an economic see-saw, 'down' at the moment, but soon to be 'up'? Is it in the early stages of an 'economic miracle', or hopelessly dumped on an entrepreneurial scrap-heap?

In contrast to the external oil shocks of the early 1970s, the policy which has become known as '**Thatcherism**' in the 1980s attempted to create 'internal shocks' to 'kick-start' life into the economy.

'Supply side economics' is a term which, during the 1980s, became generally understood to refer to a broad rage of policies aimed at improving the performance of an economy by using market forces and incentives. In the UK, to a certain extent, the term has become almost synonymous with Thatcherism.

The Thatcherite targets

The Conservative government during the 1980s approached the supply side of the economy on three broad fronts. Firstly, it tackled the labour market; secondly it changed the tax and benefit systems; and thirdly it reduced the size of the public sector. In international terms, the overall aim was to increase the **competitiveness** of the UK in relation to its main trading partners and rivals.

The main tenets of Thatcherite policy have been examined in three books in this series: *Privatization and the Public Sector* by Bryan Hurl, *Supply Side Economics* by Nigel Healey and Rosalind Levačić, and *Mrs Thatcher's Economic Legacy* by David Smith. Here, we shall concentrate on those aspects which were meant to improve the international competitiveness of the UK.

A problem with the labour market has been the shortage of **appropriate skills** in the right places at the right time. For example, when unemployment was reported to have reached two million people in 1988, there were nearly three-quarters of a million unfilled vacancies. This indicates both geographical and occupational **immobility of labour.**

In recent years various initiatives have been made in the field of education and training. The introduction of the National Curriculum in state schools in England and Wales, and the setting up of TECs (Training and Enterprise Councils), are two examples of the reorganization which has taken place. One of the duties of the TECs is to identify local skills shortages and arrange for retraining schemes for redundant workers. Whether such initiatives will have a radical effect in improving the 'flexibility' of the workforce remains very much to be seen.

Privatization and deregulation were meant to achieve many aims, including increased competitiveness and efficiency. Whether the broad aims of privatization have been fulfilled lies (in the words of Bryan Hurl) 'in the eye of the beholder'.

Supply side performance

Figure 16 shows one measure of UK supply side performance, the country's cost competitiveness. What is plotted is the 'real effective exchange rate' based on *relative unit labour costs* (RULC). The RULC is calculated by dividing average output per worker into total labour costs, and multiplying by an exchange rate index. Figure 16 would show a downward trend if the UK's trade were becoming more competitive. The fact that an upward drift is discernible in the late 1980s and early 1990s might be taken to indicate that the supply side policies of the Thatcher years have had – thus far – either a neutral effect on overall competitiveness, or have actually reduced competitiveness.

If there was really an 'economic miracle' in the 1980s, it must be asked why it is that the UK has been so badly affected by **recession.** If the supply side of the economy had really been radically altered, it must be asked why it is that the UK government has geared so much of its recent policy to the demand side. During 1989–90, in order to attempt to reduce inflation, the government raised interest rates to 15 per cent.

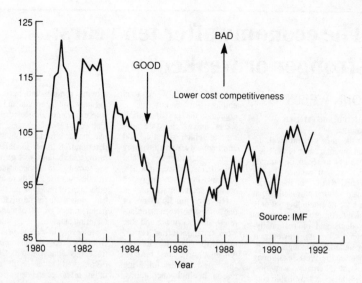

Figure 16 The UK's cost competitiveness

This was aimed at reducing demand, and it eventually led to the recession of the early 1990s. Aggregate demand went out of control in the first place as a result of financial deregulation (a supply-side policy) which made household borrowing easy, reduced saving and dramatically increased personal indebtedness, consumption and imports. By 1991 the UK had joined the EMS and was unable to reduce interest rates quickly. In the future, as the UK becomes more closely linked to a common European monetary policy, national budgetary policy will become once again the main policy instrument for offsetting purely national fluctuations in aggregate demand. Does this mean that UK plc will never shake itself free of old-fashioned Keynesian stop–go?

According to an OECD report of 1990, the UK faces years of austerity if long-term inflationary pressures are to be removed. From the point of view of UK trade and sterling, the critique by John Wells reproduced here outlines the crushing evidence for the size of the problem.

So what is it that has *not* been done on the supply side to transform the long-run performance of the country? There are many possible explanations, including the following.

Lack of investment due to 'short-termism'
UK financial institutions are accused of wanting quick profits, rather than being prepared to wait for long-term returns. Banks have preferred to finance property speculation rather than invest in industry.

The economy after ten years: stronger or weaker?

JOHN WELLS

Internal and external balance

At the most general level, the fundamental cause of the UK's inability to reconcile internal and external balance lies, as argued earlier, in the inadequate volume of traded output as a whole (including not only manufactures but also primary products and internationally-traded services). However, if we undertake a thought experiment on the 1980s, examining possible alternative scenarios, then the most reasonable conclusion to reach is that the inadequate rate of growth in manufacturing output bears the lion's share of responsibility for the inadequate level of traded output overall.

The UK manufacturing sector that has survived the Thatcher decade is certainly leaner and fitter, employing a vastly reduced labour force, more productively and much more profitably.

However, given the likely potential of the other traded sectors of the UK economy, it can be argued that the UK manufacturing sector has become too small. Britain simply does not have a large enough manufacturing sector to sustain the level of total domestic expenditure on traded and non-traded goods and services alike that would be associated with full employment.

Performance in the service industries

But, surely, the answer will come back: in today's world, we no longer need to worry if the country's manufacturing performance is relatively weak. After all, in Britain today, manufacturing now only accounts for 24% of total output and just 22% of total employment. Surely, it is argued, in the 'post-industrial' society into which we are moving, in which spending and employment are shifting away from manufactures and towards the services, it is performance in the services which counts – not manufacturing.

However, this imbalance or unevenness between manufactures and services, and the weak manufacturing performance that underlies it, does remain a grave cause for concern. And for the following reason. In employment terms, it is certainly true that Britain is becoming more of a 'post-industrial' society, as employment in the services increases both absolutely and relatively.

However, when we look at the pattern of domestic spending, there is no sign that Britain is becoming a post-industrial society, in the sense of experiencing a shift in the pattern of spending away from manufactures towards services. Taking the Thatcher decade as a whole, total domestic expenditure has risen in real terms by 26.2%. But, within that total, spending on manufactures and services has risen by roughly the same amount.

It is here that we find the reason why the poor manufacturing output record is such a cause for concern. Whilst the increase in domestic demand for services 1979–88 (of roughly 26%)was associated with a roughly equal increase in the domestic output of services (27.4%), the increase in domestic spending on manufactures (of roughly 26%) contrasts with an increase in manufacturing output of just 7.8%.

But, surely, the answer will come back: in this post-industrial society into which we are moving, is not Britain becoming increasingly specialised as a net exporter of services, especially of financial services? So that she can afford to offset any deterioration in her manufacturing trade balance with growing surpluses in service trade? In other words, that there are other areas of traded output that can compensate for the unsatisfactory rate of growth of manufacturing output.

However, in recent years, Britain's export surplus in oil trade has almost completely disappeared as a result of falling oil prices and depressed production (due, partly, to the Piper Alpha disaster). Meanwhile, Britain's balance in service trade, though it is still in surplus, has deteriorated sharply, as a result of the rapid growth of UK tourist spending abroad.

Current account deficits of this size are quite unprecedented in UK history – except, briefly, in 1974, in the immediate aftermath of OPEC's first oil price increase, when Britain was a net oil importer: a very different situation from today. At the same time as Britain is running a huge deficit on current account, it is also investing, on a massive scale, long-term abroad – to a far greater degree than foreigners are investing, long-term, in the UK. As a result, the long-term capital account registered a deficit of £13.0 bn in 1988. The sum total of these twin deficits on current and capital account in 1988 was £27.9 bn (or 6.0% of GDP), a total of quite unprecedented proportions, requiring massive short-term capital inflows (hot money inflows) to balance the books.

Source: Adapted from *Economics*, winter 1989

This is contrasted with Germany where banks often purchase equity in the firms they support, and therefore have a vested interest in long-term growth.

Lack of exchange rate flexibility
When the UK joined the ERM in 1990, there was a widely held view that it had been pegged at too high a level. This reflects the Treasury's priorities of low growth and the 'defence' of sterling, to minimize inflation.

Lack of entrepreneurial spirit
The UK has long been accused of suffering from a lack of entrepreneurial risk taking. We invented the hovercraft, and allowed other countries to benefit from its production and sale. UK management is said to be slow to adapt to new situations. It has become a cliché to state that there is no shortage of inventive flair in the UK, but very often the best British ideas have to be developed overseas. Does our educational system support the ethos of the entrepreneur, or undermine it?

Lack of investment in people
In many ways the educational 'reforms' of the 1980s are directly opposed to what is actually needed; i.e. a highly inflexible National Curriculum focusing on a list of 'subjects' which echoes the patterns of the late nineteenth and early twentieth centuries. The trend towards the publication of league tables showing the proportion of pupils gaining grades 'A' and 'B' at Advanced Level is a case in point. The ability of our schools to train our highfliers to get to university has never been a problem. What has been a problem is to provide appropriate education and training for all. Education spending has been regarded in Britain as a form of *consumption*; its 'cost' has been seen as part of the welfare system and not as a self-financing *investment*.

To quote Peter Hennessy, 'During the twentieth century, the UK has not re-tooled itself in the sense of plant and equipment, nor at the educational level.' As a schoolteacher who specializes in Economics, the present author takes no pleasure in asserting that the failure of successive governments to carry out truly *radical* reform of the educational system has proved to be not just an educational problem, not just a political problem, but a fundamental *economic* problem. The quality of domestic education affects UK trade and sterling.

KEY WORDS

Supply side   Appropriate skills
Economic growth   Immobility of labour
Thatcherism   Recession
Competitiveness   Short-termism

Reading list

Glaister, K., *The Entrepreneur*, Heinemann Educational, 1988.

Healey, N. and Levačić, R., *Supply Side Economics*, 2nd edn, Heinemann Educational, 1992.

Hennessy, P. and Anstey, C., *From Clogs to Clogs? – Britain's Relative Economic Decline Since 1851*. Strathclyde Papers on Government, University of Strathclyde, 1991.

Hurl, B., Chapter 6 in *Privatization and the Public Sector*, 2nd edn, Heinemann Educational, 1992.

Smith, D., Chapter 2 in *Mrs Thatcher's Economics: Her Legacy*, Heinemann Educational, 1992.

Turner, P., 'The postwar growth of the UK economy', *Economic Review*, September 1991.

Essay topics

1. (a) What are 'supply-side' policies? (b) Can such policies lead to an improvement in a country's economic performance? (Associated Examining Board, 1991)

2. 'Although many economists agree that the most important problems facing the UK economy lie on the 'supply side', there is much less agreement about the policies appropriate to deal with these problems'. What are the supply side problems facing the economy and why is there disagreement about the appropriate policies? (Associated Examining Board, 1989)

3. 'UK governments in the 1980s were primarily concerned about increasing incentives, generating greater competition, and eliminating market imperfections'. (a) Outline the various policies which were implemented to achieve these objectives. (b) On what criteria could the effectiveness of these policies be evaluated? (University of London School Examinations Board, 1991)

4. Use the concepts of aggregate demand and supply to analyse the effects of an increase in exports on output, employment and inflation. (University of Oxford Delegacy of Local Examinations, 1990)

Data Response Question 9

Balance of payments crisis
This task is based on a question set by the University of London School
Examinations Board in 1990. Read the extract, which is adapted from
The Times of 15 February 1988, and answer the following questions.

1. What is meant by 'UK competitiveness'?
2. Analyse the reasoning behind the statement that 'The prospect of a major balance of payments crisis remains the single most important danger for the UK economy in 1988'.
3. How may the 'strength of domestic demand in the UK relative to its trading partners' cause balance of payments problems?
4. Examine one short-term and one long-term measure likely to reduce the UK's balance of payments deficit.

The prospect of a major balance of payments crisis remains the single most important danger for the UK economy in 1988. The re-emergence of the external constraint will be increasingly important in framing monetary policy through the year.

The manufacturing deficit looks set to worsen further due to two critical factors. The first is the UK's competitiveness. The restrained growth in unit labour costs in 1987 owed a great deal to rapid productivity growth on the back of sharply expanding production. In 1988 production will grow less rapidly, productivity gains will be slow, and unit labour costs could expand sharply.

Meanwhile, the exchange rate will not be allowed to come to the rescue on present policies.

The second factor is the strength of domestic demand in the UK relative to its main trading partners. The OECD forecast real domestic demand growth of 3¾% in the UK, 2½% in the EEC as a whole and only 1% in the US. Under these circumstances the trend for the UK trade deficit has only one direction to go.'

Chapter Ten
The future: certainties and possibilities

'*A cabo de cien anos todos seremos calvos.*' (A hundred years from now we'll all be bald)   Spanish proverb

Before the year 2000, citizens of Europe will be able to receive their wages, hold bank balances, and make purchases in any shop using a single common currency. It may be called the 'ECU' or something more elegant. The banknotes and coins will vary from country to country; in the UK, for instance, we may have the monarch's head on one side, and a European emblem on the other. National currencies, such as sterling, may continue to coexist for a while, but they can expect to become redundant and whither away.

You may think that a prediction of this sort made in 1992 is just a little fanciful. But in 1972 it might have seemed fanciful to predict that the EC would soon be expanded to include not only the UK but also the newly democratized Spain, Portugal and Greece, or to predict in 1982 that within a decade South Africa would begin to dismantle apartheid, East Germany would join the EC and Russian politicians would seriously consider applying for membership of NATO.

How can we be sure that the UK will participate in a single currency? You will find the answer in Figures 17 and 18. Consider, for example, the fact that Wales has the highest concentration of Japanese firms outside Japan itself. Why does the UK attract this inward investment? Is it because of cheaper labour and employment legislation that tends to favour the employer? Possibly; but the gradual introduction of European social legislation can be expected to erode such so-called advantages. A significant reason for inward investment into the UK is the very same reason why multinationals invest in any other European country: *to gain access to the huge single market of the European Economic Area* which will be available after 1992. Eleven other members of the EC are committed to monetary union by 1998. It is surely unthinkable that the UK would stay apart and risk the wholesale movement of both real and monetary capital from this island to the continent.

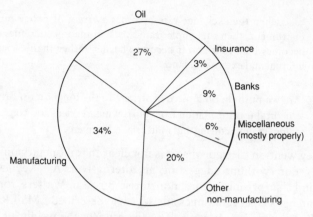

Source: *Lloyds Bank Economic Bulletin*, June 1990

Figure 17 Proportions of foreign-owned assets in broad sections of the UK economy

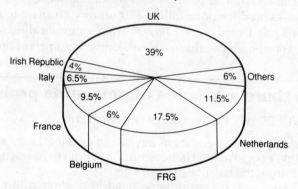

Source: US Department of Commerce

Figure 18 US direct investment by value in the EC to the end of 1988 (total = $127.8 billion)

It is perhaps ironic that this final chapter of a book with 'sterling' featured in its title is predicting the demise of sterling – the very word has a solid, indestructible feel to it, and in Latin it means 'strong'. However, it is a mistake to elevate a national currency on to a pedestal so that any adjustment of its exchange rate is seen as a blow to national virility. Such an attitude contains the seeds of its own downfall. If sterling is supported to keep it overvalued, UK industry will be uncompetitive; and if UK industry is uncompetitive, sterling will have to be supported to keep it overvalued. As Frank Hahn and Martin Weale of the University of Cambridge wrote, in a letter to *The Times* of 13 June 1991:

'. . . when the exchange rate becomes a target of policy rather than an instrument, then the whole framework of macroeconomic management becomes distorted and it becomes harder rather than easier to achieve internal and external balance.'

'Are we pushing on a piece of string? In the longer term Britain needs a structural transformation from borrowing, services and consumption – to saving, manufacturing and industrial investment.'

They went on to argue that it is not clear that monetary union offers a way out (without suggesting an alternative). As 'Keynesians' they found a surprising ally in 'monetarist' Sir Alan Walters, formerly Mrs Thatcher's chief economics adviser, who described EMS/ERM as 'half-baked' (again in a letter to *The Times*). Yet the weight of opinion in business and industry is clearly backing EMU for lower costs and greater gains on invisibles, for the City of London.

And finally, another possibility for the future. Will A-level Economics textbooks need rewriting for the 21st century, to adapt to the radicalism of Kevin Dowd (see the box)? Perhaps his radicalism will become the next orthodoxy so that we are no longer 'prisoners of the past'.

Is there a balance of payments problem?

KEVIN DOWD (*University of Nottingham*)

If I don't have a balance of payments problem, why should 56 million people in the UK have one? It is time to remove the mystique from the balance of payments.

There are three arguments used in dealing with economic issues: economic, political and non-arguments (i.e. nonsense). When dealing with the balance of payments all three are mixed together, but most arguments are political or nonsensical. They remind one of the medieval response to the 'witch problem' – the response was inappropriate and did not challenge the assumption that there was a real problem in the first place.

A country, a county, a family has to transfer funds to pay for goods and services. The latter are bought through a current account. Everything has to be paid for. The balance of payments, overall, has to be zero, only a current account deficit, which requires a corresponding surplus from a liabilities and assets account.

For the average family a whole lifetime would be constrained if it did not take on a current account deficit for, say, 25 years. This is called a mortgage and is normally regarded as a problem.

Eastern Europe must run a current account deficit in the 1990s to pull itself out of the mire, but confident in the knowledge that it can be corrected over time. Historical experience also shows that a current account is self-correcting. Nineteenth century American politicians attacked Britain for funding the USA's deficit, fearing that the USA was not paying its way and Britain's neo-colonialism would reverse the independence of 1776. Yet the USA grew to become a superpower.

This is not to argue that current account problems are non-existent. There are two possible problems. First, if a country has a fixed exchange rate then its central bank may not have enough reserves of foreign currency to defend the exchange rate. But that in itself is only a problem if the government is trying to expand aggregate demand too quickly to be compatible with the fixed exchange rate. The solution, of course, is for politicians to get their act together and pursue a consistent macroeconomic policy, but I doubt they will. The scenario for the 1990s is a return to old-style sterling crises within the ERM.

The second problem is created by politicians, the media and special-interest groups. All serious economists support free trade. The post-war growth of 1950–70 stems from the success of GATT. Economically illiterate politicians use current account deficits as an argument for protectionism. The UK has a voluntary export restraint on Japanese car imports, for example, and the USA is hysterical about Japan.

Perhaps the most effective solution is to stop collecting balance of payments data, so that the economically illiterate can find something else to worry about. Who worries about the Scottish current account? Who worries about Yorkshire's? (After all, no-one even knows what it is.)

If politicians regard a current account deficit as a problem they have failed to see the real problem – the inconsistency of their own macroeconomic policies. Why burn a witch if she is merely a harmless old maid?

This is an abridged address to Student Educational Conferences, March 1992

Reading list

Cairncross, A., 'Britain's industrial decline', *Bank of Scotland Review*, September 1988.

Crum, R., and Davies, S., Chapters 1 and 4 in *Multinationals*, Heinemann Educational, 1991.

Department of Trade and Industry, *Single Market News*, 1990.

Index